Couples Therapy for Domestic Violence

Finding Safe Solutions

Sandra M. Stith, Eric E. McCollum, and Karen H. Rosen

American Psychological Association • Washington, DC

Published by
American Psychological Association
750 First Street, NE
Washington, DC 20002
www.apa.org

To order
APA Order Department
P.O. Box 92984
Washington, DC 20090-2984
Tel: (800) 374-2721; Direct: (202) 336-5510
Fax: (202) 336-5502; TDD/TTY: (202) 336-6123
Online: www.apa.org/pubs/books
E-mail: order@apa.org

In the U.K., Europe, Africa, and the Middle East, copies may be ordered from
American Psychological Association
3 Henrietta Street
Covent Garden, London
WC2E 8LU England

Typeset in Goudy by Circle Graphics, Inc., Columbia, MD

Printer: Edwards Brothers, Inc., Ann Arbor, MI
Cover Designer: Mercury Publishing Services, Rockville, MD

The opinions and statements published are the responsibility of the authors, and such opinions and statements do not necessarily represent the policies of the American Psychological Association.

Library of Congress Cataloging-in-Publication Data

Stith, Sandra M.
Couples therapy for domestic violence : finding safe solutions / Sandra M. Stith, Eric E. McCollum, & Karen H. Rosen. — 1st ed.
      p. cm.
  Includes bibliographical references and index.
  ISBN-13: 978-1-4338-0982-8
  ISBN-10: 1-4338-0982-6
  1. Marital violence. 2. Marital violence—Prevention. I. McCollum, Eric E. II. Rosen, Karen H. III. Title.

  HV6626.S75 2011
  362.82'9253—dc22
                            2010051199

British Library Cataloguing-in-Publication Data

A CIP record is available from the British Library.

Printed in the United States of America
First Edition

doi: 10.1037/12329-000

CONTENTS

ACKNOWLEDGMENTS

A book such as this, and the clinical and research effort it represents, could not have been completed without the help of many important supporters. First, we acknowledge support from the National Institute of Mental Health in the form of a treatment development grant (Grant No. 1 R21 MH54613-02A1) to develop and pilot test the program presented here. We also acknowledge the many students and alumni from Virginia Tech who served as therapists and research assistants for the project. Domestic violence–focused couples therapy was developed in a rich community of wonderful beginning and seasoned professionals who gave of themselves to help couples stop violence. As colleagues, the three of us experienced a unique mix of stimulation and support, challenging each other to do our best work while fruitfully collaborating over many years. Finally, we owe an immeasurable debt to the clients we have met along the way. We learned more from them than we can ever adequately acknowledge about courage in the face of difficulty and the process of healing from violence.

Couples Therapy for Domestic Violence

we present ways for therapists to assess for violence more accurately, decide which couples can safely be seen together and which need to be referred for individual work or for batterer intervention services, and a framework for working with couples that both addresses danger and uses the existing strengths in couples' relationships as the basis for change. We know that couples treatment remains controversial in the field of intimate partner violence (IPV). Thoughtful practitioners worry about potential risks to safety and the erosion of personal responsibility if couples are seen together. We take these concerns seriously. We also know, however, that a growing body of research findings supports the use of couples treatment and indicates no greater danger from this approach than from others common in the field. We also know that many couples seek couples therapy as part of their efforts to end the violence in their relationships and find a more peaceful and satisfying life together. Our approach is not simply traditional marital therapy with an awareness of violence added in the margins. As you will see throughout the book, we have made significant efforts to provide skilled assessment at the beginning of treatment, structural modifications to treatment sessions, and ongoing monitoring throughout to increase the safety of our clients as much as we can.

DVFCT was developed collaboratively after the three coauthors (Stith, McCollum, and Rosen) began working together as faculty in the Marriage and Family Therapy Program at Virginia Tech's Washington, D.C.–area campus in the early 1990s. Each of us brought different lenses to the issue. Stith had worked in a shelter for victims of IPV and had conducted a series of studies seeking to understand male IPV offenders. McCollum came to the topic after having developed a treatment manual and providing clinical supervision in a randomized clinical trial examining a couples approach to treating women's substance abuse. Rosen had studied victims of violence: how they became entrapped in violent relationships and how they were able to leave those relationships. In 1991, Stith, Rosen, Barasch, and Wilson conducted a small study at the university clinic and learned that although only 12% of the couples who came to therapy were originally identified as having experienced IPV, slightly more than 40% had actually been physically violent to their partners. When we became aware of how much IPV our students were actually treating, we began to augment our student's training with specific information about IPV and to enhance our protocol for screening for violence. We were concerned that traditional marital therapy when a couple had experienced IPV might be dangerous, so we began to develop a treatment approach based on our knowledge of the literature on IPV and our clinical experiences as couples therapists.

In 1997, we received funding from the National Institute of Mental Health to develop and pilot test our treatment program. We used a variety of standardized research measures to examine the effectiveness of our program, but we also wanted to learn from our clients and our therapists as we refined and developed the program. (Results of this research are presented in the final chapter of the book.) In the early phase of our project, we conducted individual interviews with our clients after the second, fifth, and final treatment session to learn about their experiences. We contacted clients who had completed therapy or who had dropped out of treatment to learn from them how we might improve DVFCT and what was most helpful and unhelpful to them. We interviewed many of our project therapists and asked for their feedback as well. Finally, at the end of each session, we asked clients to complete a weekly session feedback form, giving us their impression of the helpfulness of that specific session. We used all of this data to make major changes to DVFCT over the course of its development. Our original treatment manual differs greatly from the book presented here. We also use quotes from these research interviews throughout this book to help the reader understand the perspective of the clients in our program. We hope that their voices will help our readers get a picture of the strengths of couples who struggle with IPV as well as the suffering they must sometimes endure.

The book begins with an overview of the historical context of IPV treatment, objections to couples treatment in the wake of IPV, and why we believe couples treatment can be useful. In the second chapter, we discuss clinical assessment and screening for appropriateness of conjoint treatment of violent couples. The third chapter presents an overview of the first 6 weeks of the program, which we defined as therapist-directed. During the first 6 weeks, much of the treatment is separated by gender (either men's and women's groups or individuals). The next six chapters address specific aspects of treatment during each of the first 6 weeks. Chapters 10 and 11 provide an overview of the conjoint phase of treatment. In Chapter 12, we describe some of the clients who have participated in our program in the hope that their stories will help this work come alive for the reader. The final chapter of this book presents results of research conducted on the model.

DVFCT, as we have developed and used it, is delivered in two formats: in multicouple groups and with individual couples. In both formats, we use cotherapists. As we illustrate in the following chapters, we find that having two therapists in the session gives us more flexibility in dealing with crises, increases the kinds of interventions we can provide, and helps defuse the often emotionally intense interactions that couples have when dealing with the levels of conflict that have brought them to our treatment. We are certainly aware, however, that using cotherapists adds significant cost to providing therapy and may not be financially feasible in some settings. We have trained many professionals in this model and have heard from some of them that they have successfully adapted DVFCT for use with one therapist when working with individual couples. In place of concurrent meetings between each partner and a cotherapist, at the beginning and end of sessions, for instance, one therapist can meet separately first with one partner and then with the other. The psychoeducational material in the first six sessions of DVFCT can be delivered to each partner in separate sessions.

Adapting DVFCT for use by one therapist may be possible for the individual couple format, but we feel strongly that cotherapists are needed in the multicouple group. The complexity of the interactions in a group made up of couples, the possibility that an individual or couple may need crisis management while the other couples need to be seen for a regular session, and the potential for cotherapists to model new and more successful interactions all suggest to us that cotherapists are needed in group. Fortunately, the cost of cotherapists can be more easily offset in couples group therapy. The outcome findings that we present later in the book are all based on a cotherapy model, and we have only anecdotal reports that DVFCT is successfully adaptable for delivery by one therapist. Traditionally, we have delivered DVFCT with a team comprising an advanced graduate trainee and a licensed professional. Readers who wish to use our model in their agency or practice might consider partnering with a graduate program if providing cotherapy seems cost prohibitive. Regardless of how a practitioner decides to deliver DVFCT, we remain convinced that all decisions about treatment must be made with safety first in mind.

1

THE CHANGING FACE OF INTIMATE PARTNER VIOLENCE TREATMENT

There's not hardly anyone that would take a violent couple. . . . I've called and you just get "if he needs counseling call this number" . . . not even churches. There's nobody that wants to deal with violent couples. All they want to say is, "Well, how soon do you want a divorce?" Well, I'd really like to try to work it out first.

—A client in our program

The statement above, by a woman whom we saw early in our work with couples who had physically assaulted one another, exemplifies the prevailing attitude toward conjoint couples therapy in the wake of violence. Couples who seek counseling together to work on violence in their relationship are usually met with resistance from professionals who believe that treating violent couples together will result in a variety of dangerous outcomes.

COUPLES THERAPY IN HISTORICAL CONTEXT

Before the feminist movement in the 1970s, violence in the home was considered largely a private matter. In the 1970s, a group of feminist activists, led by individuals such as Erin Pizzey and Susan Schecter, worked to develop a grassroots movement to change the acceptability of wife beating and to provide safety and shelter for female victims of violence. The shelter movement was successful in bringing the issue of male partner violence into the public dialogue and began offering a safe, but temporary, respite for victims of this violence. Eventually it became clear that simply providing a safe haven for victims was not enough. The work needed to focus not only on providing safety for victims but also on holding men accountable for their behavior and on helping them to stop being violent.

In their emphasis on holding men accountable for their violence, as well as their concern about men's use of the privileges of a patriarchal society to maintain unfair advantage over their female partners, early women's advocates adopted a feminist lens that saw all violence emanating from culturally reinforced male power. They argued that couples therapy would further oppress women who found themselves not only physically assaulted but also emotionally dominated by their male partners. This was not an unreasonable concern. Workers in women's shelters are only too familiar with victims of violence whose fear of their male partners can only be described as frank terror. Victims' fears were often not misplaced. The prevalence of women being seriously injured and killed by their male partners remains sobering. Tjaden and Thoennes (1998) found that 22% of women experienced violence in their current or previous relationship and 42% of these women sustained injury due to intimate partner violence (IPV). In addition, 8.8% of these women were hospitalized for injury due to IPV. Aside from concerns about safety, victim advocates also argued that asking women to participate in couples counseling with their abusive partners implied that the women had some responsibility for the assault— a tactic often employed by the men themselves to excuse their behavior. Every men's group leader has heard more than once: "If the bitch would just learn to shut up when I tell her to, I wouldn't end up hitting her. She just doesn't learn." Susan Schechter, in her 1987 *Guide for Mental Health Practitioners in Domestic Violence*, published by the National Coalition Against Domestic Violence, stated that

> couples therapy is an inappropriate intervention that further endangers the woman. It encourages the abuser to blame the victim by examining her "role" in his problem. By seeing the couple together, the therapist erroneously suggests that the partner, too, is responsible for the abuser's behavior. (p. 16)

Advocates expressed other concerns. Women might be lulled into a false sense of security, for instance, when their partners agree to participate in therapy, taking their participation as an indication of readiness to tackle difficult relationship issues calmly. Believing this, they might bring up issues that could shame their partners or anger them, leading to increased tension and the threat of retaliation when they leave the relative safety of the therapist's office. Other concerns that have been expressed about conjoint treatment include the possibility that a victim might be intimidated or fearful and not be comfortable sharing her concerns in a room with her partner, thus putting her in the bind of either angering her partner or "lying," as it were, to the therapist.

Given their concerns about victim safety and their conviction that all violence in intimate heterosexual relationships arose from male power and its misuse, early workers in the field of domestic violence urged strong legal sanctions against men who assaulted their partners and a treatment approach that separated men and women. The goal of gender-specific (i.e., separate) treatment was to vigorously confront male efforts to accept anything less than their total responsibility for their violent actions and attack their often unconscious use of male privilege while separately empowering female victims to protect themselves and, it was hoped, to leave the abusive relationship. This model remains common today across the country.

PREVAILING MODEL FOR TREATING DOMESTIC VIOLENCE

Group treatment for male offenders is required or recommended in nearly all state offender standards. Although the emphasis on accountability remains prominent in most offender intervention programs, most programs tend to use an eclectic set of interventions. Many still focus on teaching men about the negative effects of constricted male roles through sex-role resocialization and increasing men's awareness of control tactics so that they will be more aware of their abusive behaviors and will have increased empathy for victims. However, other programs have expanded their focus and teach offenders skills to replace destructive behaviors, work to help men change faulty patterns of thinking that lead to negative feelings and abusive behaviors, or help men deal with childhood experiences, attachment injuries, and shame through trauma-based approaches. Whereas male offenders are typically required to attend treatment by a judge or a probation officer, female partners' participation remains voluntary.

In the shadow of the assertion that couples therapy will increase the risk to victims, clinicians, state certification bodies, and policymakers have opted for the presumably safer standard treatment of gender-specific groups for male batterers and female victims. Currently, 43 states have developed guidelines for offender treatment (Maiuro & Eberle, 2008). The majority of these guidelines explicitly prohibit any type of couples sessions or therapy during the course of the primary domestic violence intervention for court-ordered offenders. The remaining state guidelines either say nothing to exclude or limit such sessions or allow supplemental sessions to be conducted subject to particular conditions "after a specified period of time, when the perpetrator has been violence-free or when victim safety is properly assessed and reasonably assured (California, Colorado, Illinois, Kansas, Nevada, Rhode Island, Washington, West Virginia)" (Maiuro & Eberle, 2008, p. 128). In some state guidelines, the partner may participate in joint sessions with the perpetrator only with the proviso that "the sessions not be conducted as traditional couple's therapy in which joint responsibility for violence and abuse may be implied or assumed" (p. 3).

WHY DO COUPLES TREATMENT?

Given that a widely agreed-on treatment for domestic violence already existed and was, in fact, often legally mandated and that couples treatment was seen as both dangerous and oppressive to women, what led us to set out in the early 1990s to explore how to work with men and women together to end the violence in their relationships? There were a number of reasons why we decided to work with IPV in a relational context. In part the evidence suggested to us that the concerns about couples treatment were exaggerated, and in part we believed that couples treatment could be an important and useful addition to the overall community response to IPV. We felt that the philosophical objections to systems treatment were unfounded, that our definition and understanding of IPV was changing from a political framework to a scientific framework, that the failure to pay attention to the relationship when violence occurred left both men and women vulnerable, and that the "one size fits all" treatment of male batterer intervention did not work nearly as well as was hoped when it was instituted in the early 1970s. In addition, we came to believe that that violence can end, relationships can be improved, and women and men both can be empowered through the careful application of conjoint couples treatment.

Systemic Perception of Violence

In our view, the primary philosophical objection to couples treatment—that a systemic approach blames the victim and relieves the perpetrator of responsibility for his acts—is based on a simplistic and outdated understanding of systems models (McCollum & Stith, 2008). Simplistic circular causality models of interaction have given way to more complex and layered models—models that include the individual and the social context along with the interactions between partners (see, e.g., Breunlin, Schwartz, & MacKune-Karrer, 1992, for a general systems model that integrates various levels from the intrapsychic to the cultural). Sprenkle (1994) argued that few, if any, systemic family therapists would consider a woman's actions the cause for her partner's violence against her, nor would they eschew taking a firm stand against violence in favor of "systemic neutrality." The model we describe in this book has operationalized this theoretical position. We seek both to hold violent partners accountable and to intervene to change couple interaction.

In support of this viewpoint, Wileman and Wileman (1995) found that reductions in violence were associated with both the man assuming responsibility for his own violence and with the woman decreasing her vulnerability and taking an active role in balancing power in the relationship, one of the primary goals of our treatment model.

Maintaining the Safety of the Victim

With regard to the second objection raised by opponents of conjoint treatment—that conjoint treatment endangers victims—research in the field shows no increased physical danger to women in couples treatment when that treatment specifically addresses domestic violence (Brannen & Rubin, 1996; Dunford, 2000; O'Leary, Heyman, & Neidig, 1999; Stith, Rosen, & McCollum, 2002b; Stith, Rosen, McCollum, & Thomsen, 2004). For example, our research, which is described in detail later in this book, indicates that couples participating in our program had a significant reduction in both male-to-female and female-to-male violence after completing treatment and that members of a no-treatment comparison group did not change in their levels of violence. Furthermore, Dunford (2000) and O'Leary et al. (1999) both found no differences in treatment outcome for couples in treatment compared with men only in treatment. In discussing their findings, O'Leary et al. also addressed some of the concerns about conjoint treatment. The authors indicated that

> compared to wives in the GST [gender-specific treatment], wives in the conjoint treatment were not fearful of participating with their husbands; were not fearful during the sessions; did not blame themselves for the violence; and were not put at an increased risk for violence during the program. (p. 494)

The authors further suggested that "at this point, both conjoint treatment and GSTs for wife abuse appear to be equally viable modes of intervention" (p. 501). Finally, a study by Fals-Stewart, Kashdan, O'Farrell, and Bircher (2002) found that couples therapy for substance abuse was more effective than individual therapy for substance abuse in reducing domestic violence, even though violence was not the target of treatment.

Furthermore, although male treatment groups are effective in eliminating violence for some men, negative effects from men's groups have been described in the literature (Edleson & Tolman, 1992). Some group members support other members' negative attitudes about women or implicitly or explicitly support a man's use of abusive behavior. Although Tolman's (1990) qualitative research indicated that most men in batterer intervention programs reported that the group experience was an important ingredient in bringing about change, some women partners in Tolman's study described negative group effects. For example, one woman said her spouse came home and told her she should stop complaining because other men beat their wives much worse than he did. The potential for negative male bonding in abuse groups is another potential problem with the standard treatment format (Hart, 1988). We found unintended consequences of male-only treatment among our own study participants. When we began offering couples treatment, we required that the male offenders complete a batterer intervention program before beginning our program. Women in our program told us that, in their view, one of the most dangerous times of the week for them while the men were in batterers treatment was when the men returned home after men's group. The men were often angry and resentful that they were required to attend the program and were often distressed by intense discussions that occurred in the group or by their experiences of shame, leaving the women feeling at increased risk of verbal or physical assault. Women in our program also told us that their partners deliberately misrepresented what they were learning in the group and that they felt left out of the process. Men would come back from group and tell their partners that they had been encouraged to leave if they got angry and that their partner should allow them to leave for as long as it took, even if it were several days. The women sometimes felt that the group was not helping them feel safer or their partners become more in control.

Cause of Violence

The idea that violence in relationships is caused primarily by the patriarchal nature of society in which men assault women to exert control and women's violence is either self-defense or inconsequential is also being called into question. As the advocacy movement succeeded in making the much-needed case that IPV is a serious social problem deserving of society's attention and resources, two things occurred. First, our cultural definition of violence that deserved social sanction began to expand. We are currently seeing both men and women court-ordered to treatment for acts of aggression that would have barely drawn a reprimand by the police 20 years ago. Second, as the need for political persuasion has decreased, a different kind of conversation about IPV has emerged—a conversation that is less absolutist and confrontational and that relies on scientific understanding more than political understanding as its foundation. Thus, we are coming to understand that not all violence springs from frank efforts of power and control and that women initiate aggression as well as defend themselves. In fact, most research has found that women initiate and carry out physical assaults on their partners as often as do men (Archer, 2002; Stith & Straus, 1995). In our initial project to develop the treatment program described in this book, we only accepted couples in which the male was ostensibly the sole offender. However, almost 90% of the female partners self-reported that they had also used physical violence in the relationship. If reciprocal violence is taking place in relationships, treating men without treating women is not likely to stop it. In fact, cessation of partner violence by one partner is highly dependent on whether the other partner also stops hitting (Feld & Straus, 1989; Gelles & Straus, 1988). One of our male clients, whose wife also reported using violence, indicated the following in an interview with one of our researchers:

> I have two goals. My first goal is to take care of myself, and that's pretty obvious. My wife believes that as long as I'm angry, that affects our relationship. The only way I'm going to make the relationship work is I have to make the initial action. I accept that. If I learn to control my anger, and she starts seeing that, boom. Half the marriage is resolved. Second goal . . . I want her to recognize her own anger. But I've got to do something about myself first. I have to accept that responsibility.

Clearly, the difference in physical strength between most men and women means that the largest proportion of assaults that result in physical injury are perpetrated by men (Archer, 2002; Tjaden & Thoennes, 1998; U.S. Department of Justice, 2002). However, despite the much lower probability of physical injury resulting from attacks by women, women's violence is serious, just as it would be serious if men "only" slapped their wives or "only" slapped female coworkers (Straus, 1993). Additionally, when women use violence in relationships, they are at greater risk of being severely assaulted by their partners (Feld & Straus, 1989; Gondolf, 1998). Thus, attention to the violent acts of both partners is necessary to help couples leave treatment safe and violence-free.

Not All Partner Violence Is the Same

As society have moved from a political to a more scientific understanding of IPV, some of the other existing assumptions about violence have been called into question. Whereas early advocates maintained that all violence in heterosexual relationships was based on the assertion of male power and privilege, current research has made it clear that male batterers are a heterogeneous group (Gondolf, 1988; Saunders, 1992; Stuart & Holtzworth-Munroe, 1995). Holtzworth-Munroe and Stuart (1994) reviewed the research on types of relationally violent men and reported that three descriptive dimensions (i.e., severity of marital violence, generality of violence [toward the wife or toward others], and presence of psychopathology and personality disorders) have consistently been found to distinguish subtypes of batterers. They suggest that three subtypes of batterers exist—family only, dysphoric–borderline, and generally violent or antisocial—and that tailoring treatment to each subtype of violent men might improve treatment outcome. Stuart and Holtzworth-Munroe (1995) hypothesized that family-only batterers are likely to be the least violent of the groups and that they are likely to have developed problems such as insecure attachment patterns, mild social skills deficits, and low levels of impulsivity. They further hypothesized that this type of batterer may be the most appropriate for couple's treatment:

> Family-only batterers tend to have stable marriages characterized by rel-atively high marital satisfaction and a high level of commitment to the relationship. Thus, couple therapy may be appropriate if the violence is not severe (independently verified by the female partner) and both part-ners are highly motivated to improve the relationship. (p. 168)

More recently, M. P. Johnson and colleagues (M. P. Johnson, 1995, 2000; Johnson & Ferraro, 2000) began to investigate different patterns of vio-lence in relationships. Instead of looking at different types of perpetrators, they have studied the different relational dynamics surrounding violence and describe four relational patterns. *Intimate terrorism* is primarily found in stud-ies examining court-involved batterers and is described as an asymmetric pat-tern in which violent and nonviolent acts are motivated by a perpetrator's desire to gain broad control over his or her partner. Although intimate terror-ism was originally conceived of as primarily a male pattern characterized by the pervasive domination and control that one partner has over the other, more recent research has suggested that both males and females are responsi-ble for intimate terrorism (Coker et al., 2002; Graham-Kevan & Archer, 2005; Henderson, Bartholomew, Trinke, & Kwong, 2005). In some cases, actual vio-lent assaults have not occurred for years, but the mere history and threat of such assaults maintain the perpetrator's near total control of his partner. We have seen women literally "shaking in their boots" at the prospect of meeting with a partner who fits the intimate terrorism pattern even when they have not been physically assaulted for years. (As we explain later, such couples are not, in our view, appropriate for couples treatment.) *Violent resistance* is a pat-tern of violence in which the victim, using nonviolent and violent acts, retal-iates against a partner's attempts to control him or her. Victims in this category may be using violence, but they are using violence for self-defense. *Mutual vio-lent control* is a symmetric pattern of violence in which both partners use vio-lent and nonviolent acts to exert control over one another. M. P. Johnson and Ferraro (2000) characterized partners who engage in this type of violence as "two intimate terrorists" wrestling for general control of the relationship. Most germane for our discussion of couples treatment is M. P. Johnson and Ferraro's category of *situational couple violence*.

Situational couple violence is an intermittent pattern of violence perpetrated by either one partner (i.e., asymmetrical) or both partners (i.e., symmetrical) in response to occasional conflicts. In contrast to intimate terrorism, situational violence does not spring from an overarching and pervasive effort to control one's partner. Instead, it is motivated by the desire to control a specific situation (M. P. Johnson, 1995, 2000; M. P. Johnson & Ferraro, 2000). M. P. Johnson (1995) described situational couple violence as a couple dynamic in which conflicts may unintentionally escalate to minor violence but rarely escalate to severe, life-threatening violence. There is lower per-couple frequency of violence in this type of violence than in intimate terrorism. In addition, men are no more likely to initiate violent conflicts than women, and women are more likely to report patterns of mutual violence and retaliation against male perpetrators (M. P. Johnson, 1995, 2000; Milardo, 1998). Couples who experience situational violence are less likely to seek assistance from shelters, report incidents to police, file for a divorce, or seek medical attention. And while fear in the specific situation may be present, there is no pervasive sense of fear or domination. Situational violence is hypothesized to be the most prevalent type of relationship violence, particularly within samples from the general population, and, as recent research suggests, in couples seeking conjoint therapy (Simpson, Doss, Wheeler, & Christensen, 2007). In fact, M. P. Johnson (2006), when describing situational violence suggested that "the core problem is one of communication skill deficiencies for which an individual compensates with verbal aggression that then escalates into violence" (p. 18). Most of the violence in national random surveys such as the National Family Violence Survey or in couples seeking therapy is situational couple violence.

What does the growing domestic violence typology literature reveal about the use of couples treatment? The fact that couples who engage in violence are heterogeneous groups underscores the importance of viewing IPV within a relationship context and distinguishing among different types of couples who engage in IPV. Furthermore, this literature suggests that the typical strategy of prescribing the same intervention for all cases of IPV (male-only profeminist psychoeducation) may not be sound. M. P. Johnson's work, in particular, suggests that a significant portion of IPV springs from relationship conflict, leading us to conclude that efforts to change relationship dynamics may be the most appropriate treatment for a carefully selected subset of couples in which there has been violence. Indeed, the treatment program described in this book is most appropriate for one subtype of IPV: couples engaging in situational couple violence. Because we recognize that different types of violence exist, we have found that terms such as *victim*, *perpetrator*, or *battering*, are generally not appropriate for couples who engage in symmetrical situational couple violence.

Problems With Traditional Treatment

Sadly, the hope that male-only batterer intervention alone or in combination with victim support services would consistently help men become nonabusive in their relationships has not been borne out. We have a number of concerns about an across-the-board prescription of men's batterer intervention or anger management groups as the only treatment approach for IPV. First, the ability of such groups actually to help men stop violence has not been sufficiently demonstrated. Babcock, Green, and Robie (2004) conducted a meta-analysis of batterer intervention outcome studies and found that such programs offered little benefit over simple arrest. When outcome is measured on the basis of the report of the man's partner (i.e., the woman reports whether or not he has been violent again after arrest or treatment), previous research finds a rather small effect size for treatment. Babcock et al. noted, "To a clinician, this means that a woman is 5% less likely to be reassaulted by a man who was arrested, sanctioned, and went to a batterers' program than by a man who was simply arrested and sanctioned" (p. 1044). We do not take this finding to mean that batterer intervention groups are useless or that no one ever receives benefit from them. Rather, we take this to mean that we must work to develop effective and cost-effective batterer intervention treatments and that we must also look to other treatment approaches to combat the difficult issue of violence in intimate relationships.

In addition to our concerns about the effectiveness of gender-specific treatment approaches, we are also concerned about the lack of focus on relational dynamics that results from such strategies. Of course, this was a primary motivation for using gender-separate treatment to begin with because early women's advocates feared that a focus on relational issues would inherently blame and disempower women. However, we are concerned that not examining relationship issues for some couples may result in less than optimal treatment. Although single-gender treatment groups address an offender's role in IPV, they do not address any underlying relationship dynamics that may influence each partner's decision to remain in the relationship or that may play a part in maintaining the violence. The holistic approach that results from systems theory emphasizes the importance of examining not only characteristics of individuals involved in the violent relationship but also the dynamics that occur within the relational context. By examining relational patterns, we do not mean to suggest that patterns of relating cause violence. The responsibility for violence, or for any other act, remains with the originator of that act. However, relational patterns may make it more or less likely that an act may recur in the future.

The role of marital distress illustrates the usefulness of a systemic view in understanding vulnerability to violence. In a study involving the prediction of mild and severe husband-to-wife physical aggression with 11,870 randomly selected military personnel, Pan, Neidig, and O'Leary (1994) found that marital discord was the most accurate predictor of physical aggression against a partner. For every 20% increase in marital discord, the odds of mild spouse abuse increased by 102%, and the odds of severe spouse abuse increased by 183%. In addition, Straus and Yodanis (1996) found that relationship conflict tripled the odds of wife-to-husband physical assault. Because relationship discord is a strong predictor of physical aggression toward a partner, it would seem that failure to address relationship problems at some point in the treatment of men or women would leave couples more vulnerable to reexperiencing violence.

Even if we could not demonstrate that relationship dynamics influence the occurrence of violence, there are still compelling reasons to provide conjoint treatment to some couples in which partners have assaulted one another. We must recognize that violence does not necessarily mean the demise of the relationship. In fact, abuse is often chronic and recurrent. Many women do not want to leave their violent partners; they want the violence to end. It is estimated that between 21% and 80% of women remain with their abusive partners or return to them after leaving a women's shelter even when severe violence or injury might have occurred (Sullivan, Basta, Tan, & Davidson, 1992; Sullivan & Rumptz, 1994). They continue to live with their partners and need a safe forum to both work on ending the violence and deal with the many contentious issues that may arise in daily life that could give rise to violence—extended family problems, financial worries, parenting issues, and so forth.

Failing to provide services to both parties in an ongoing relationship may disadvantage the couple that chooses to stay together. Interviews with clients participating in our treatment program illustrate the importance of including both partners in treatment at some time. For example, one male client expressed his view of the strengths and limitations of the men's group:

> [Men's groups] can't really address relationships because they're only seeing one half of the issue. . . . The primary function was to persuade the people to stop [violence] and give them tools to help them do that. However, I mean, that was good, that was right, that's what they should be doing. The other side of that is these people are involved in relationships and there may have been something wrong with the relationship. Yes, it was a bad attribute of the guy's behavior, but there was something else there too, and that needs to, at some point be addressed.

A female client who participated in a battered women's support group before beginning our program expressed her perspective on the importance of conjoint therapy:

> You go into an isolated group of women. . . . We all talked a lot. But we're just in there supporting each other and saying how wrong [things are] . . . this doesn't feel right, this doesn't feel good. Pointing out the

things that aren't right. That escalates . . . It's like they're building each other up. But separately. [The men] are getting support in the [anger management] program to feel better about themselves, maybe to help control the anger. In the women's support group they're getting support to build them up. But what are you doing for the couple? . . . Doing this in a vacuum, for us was not working. I don't know how it can with anyone. Someone just attending the [anger management] program and . . . not having any interaction with the women. It was like one-sided. My going to [victim's support group], I got support there, but when I tried to communicate what I was learning from [it] there was resistance [by my partner]. It was like we weren't in the same show.

Finally, we developed this program because we believed that therapists needed it. Many therapists we have spoken to who work with couples and families report that they rarely, if ever, see a couple that has been violent to one another. Rather than reflecting a truth about the clients they see, we understand this to reflect a truth about therapists. IPV is more prevalent in regular clinical practice than many clinicians realize. Couples often do not talk about violence in their relationship, and therapists do not ask the specific questions needed to uncover this information. Failure to assess adequately for violence leaves both partners at risk and the therapist unaware of a major detriment to marital functioning. After reviewing the existing studies, Jose and O'Leary (2009) reported that between 36% and 58% of women seeking outpatient treatment reported being physically abused by their male partner in the year before assessment, and between 37% and 57% of men reported an assault by a female partner. Even when psychotherapists believe that they do not treat people involved in domestic violence, it is unlikely that this is the case. It is more likely that the violence has remained hidden because the therapist has not clearly assessed for it. One barrier to assessment may be that psychotherapists are unprepared to deal with violence should they encounter it and that they therefore do not ask careful questions about its presence. In fact, Todahl, Linville, Chou, and Cosenza (2008) found that students in a graduate program that emphasized universal screening for IPV often chose not to screen because they lacked confidence in their ability to address violence effectively in the therapeutic context. Thus, another reason that we developed this treatment program was to give therapists who are seeing couples experiencing violence a way to confidently assess the level of violence occurring in the families they are seeing and to provide a treatment program designed to address both IPV and relationship as safely as possible.

Although couples treatment is controversial and we agree that not all couples who have experienced violence in their relationship should be seen conjointly, we are also convinced that a specific group of violent couples can use and benefit from a thoughtful couples counseling approach. That group includes couples who have experienced mild-to-moderate violence, who want to stay in their relationship, and who want to end the violence between them. This book presents a safety-oriented, domestic violence–focused approach to working with such couples that is the result of more than 10 years of development and testing, funded in part by a grant from the National Institute of Mental Health.

Our approach diverges significantly from regular approaches to couples therapy. Extra safeguards need to be incorporated into the work to manage the risks. We chose to base our model on the solution-focused brief therapy model (SFBT; for a complete description, see de Shazer, et al., 2007), which does not depend on raising emotional intensity, asking clients to interact directly with one another, or understanding the historical roots of conflicts. SFBT instead attempts to elucidate areas of strength and competence in our clients' relationships and use these as building blocks for a more satisfied and abuse-free future. In addition, we have significantly modified the structure of our sessions, meeting individually with each partner at each session and keeping selected secrets when we believe that revealing them would put partners at risk (Rosen, Matheson, Stith, & McCollum, 2003; Stith, McCollum, Rosen, Locke, & Goldberg, 2005; Stith, Rosen, & McCollum, 1999, 2002a; Tucker, Stith, Howell, McCollum, & Rosen, 2000). Further, we developed and tested our treatment program in two different formats: a cotherapy team with individual couples and a cotherapy team with a multicouple group. This book describes both approaches and tries to make clear the ways treatment is similar or different using the two different modalities.

Therapists working with IPV using our approach face a number of challenges. They must be knowledgeable about domestic violence, couples treatment, and solution-oriented treatment. We believe our program can best be delivered by licensed mental health providers who have had training and supervision in couples therapy and especially in working with high-intensity couples. It is also expected that they have some level of familiarity with the dynamics and treatment of domestic violence. We present some basic strategies and ideas in these fields, but it is beyond the scope of this book to provide all the information needed to treat violent couples safely and effectively. Additional resources are suggested in the Suggested Readings section.

Despite the controversy about couples treatment for IPV and the challenges that therapists who take on this difficult subject face, we remain convinced that there is much benefit for our clients if we try to help them, even when the risk of violence and abuse hang in the air. Over and over again, we have seen defeated and hurt human beings begin to blossom as a result of our careful confidence that they, as a couple, can find a better way to be together, or a safe way to part. No couple has ever left our treatment free of problems, but many have left free of violence and abuse and happier with their lives in general.

2

ASSESSMENT FOR INTIMATE PARTNER VIOLENCE AND SCREENING FOR INCLUSION IN THE TREATMENT PROGRAM

This chapter provides guidance to help couples therapists (a) identify when violence is occurring in a relationship, (b) understand the lethality of the violence, and (c) determine whether a couple is appropriate for conjoint treatment. In our model, assessment involves two stages. First, we assess all couples for domestic violence, even when the couple does not present it as an issue. Again, given that almost 70% of couples who come for regular outpatient care have experienced at least one violent episode, careful assessment of all couples is imperative. When we find any indication that violence might be occurring in a relationship, we use a more thorough screening assessment to determine whether the couple is appropriate for our treatment program and also to determine the potential lethality of the violence.

WHY UNIVERSAL SCREENING OF ALL COUPLES IS NEEDED

Unfortunately, therapists often fail to identify abuse even in the context of clear evidence given by their clients. Hansen, Harway, and Cervantes (1991) asked family therapists to respond to vignettes with obvious evidence of severe violence. However, 40% of the therapists failed to recognize the abuse and therefore would have left the abuse untreated. More recent research is somewhat more encouraging. Schacht, Dimidjian, George, and Berns (2009) surveyed 620 couples therapists and found that 53% reported conducting universal screening—that is, they screened all couples treated in the past year for the presence of domestic violence. However, their approaches to screening left much to be desired. Most respondents did not consistently interview both partners separately, and more than three fourths did not use written questionnaires during the screening process. We hope that this chapter helps couples therapists understand the recommended procedures for assessing for violence in relationships, regardless of whether they use the treatment model described in this book.

Clients have various reasons for not reporting the presence of violence in their relationships (Aldarondo & Straus, 1994). They may believe that violence is acceptable or tolerable and therefore not an important issue to bring up in therapy. Clients involved in severe forms of violence may be fearful of potential repercussions from their partner if they tell the therapist. Clients consumed with shame and humiliation are particularly in danger of not telling anyone, including their therapist, about the violence. Every client is different and will have his or her own reasons for not reporting or for underreporting the occurrence of violence, but it is the therapist's responsibility to use appropriate techniques to assess for partner violence.

Therapists fail to identify the occurrence of domestic violence in their clients' relationships for a variety of reasons (Aldarondo & Straus, 1994). First and foremost, many therapists do not ask about abuse. Sometimes therapists do not ask about abuse because they don't know how to ask; sometimes they do not ask because they would not know what to do if the client says there had been abuse; and sometimes they do not ask because they take one look at their client and think their clients do not look like people who would be violent.

We believe it is critical for therapists to screen all couples for domestic violence.

INTAKE INTERVIEWS AND FORMS

The first step in assessing partner violence is to determine whether any aggression is occurring in the relationship. This assessment should take place with every couple being seen and should include both an oral interview and a written assessment instrument. It is important that interviews regarding potential interpersonal violence be held with each partner separately. Neither partner may feel comfortable or safe disclosing the abuse in the presence of their partner. When each person is asked privately about their own and their partner's violence, the therapist is able to consider each person's story and the consensus or lack of consensus between stories. Therapists can increase the odds that violence will be detected by paying attention to the language they use in asking about potential violence. Asking a couple about how conflict is handled in their relationship and what happens when they get angry or in a fight is more likely to result in violence being detected than asking directly about violence or abuse. Also, asking about shoving, pushing, and grabbing is more likely to result in an admission by clients than is asking about "violence."

Our experience is that most of our clients do not consider "shoving," "pushing," or "grabbing" as being violent behavior. In fact, one client who reported that both he and his partner pushed, grabbed, and kicked each other said,

> If you're looking for people, like violent people, man, we are not it! You know a few little kicks and stuff here and there, with no more than people do when they are playing. We are not violent. We don't do one another when we are fighting and stuff.

Later he said, "Psychologically I beat her, but I don't beat her physically." It seemed clear from the reports of many of our clients, that they did not believe that the aggressive acts they reported constituted violence; therefore, it is important that therapists ask about specific acts rather than about "violence."

Although each client is unique, some questions the therapist might ask include:

- "What happens when you and your partner argue?"
- "Do you ever feel unsafe at home?"
- "Have you ever been physically hurt or felt threatened?"
- "Have you ever been or are you currently concerned about harming your partner?"
- "Have you ever felt afraid of your partner?"
- "Has your partner ever:
  - pushed, grabbed, slapped, choked or kicked you?
  - forced you to have sex or made you do sexual things you didn't want to?
  - Threatened to hurt you, your children, or someone close to you?
  - Stalked, followed, or monitored you?"

In addition to asking all clients in separate interviews about how they handle conflict and about specific acts of aggression, we also include general questions in our intake form that all clients complete when seeking services at our clinic. These questions include: "Does anyone in this family have concerns about the way anger is handled? If so, explain." Or, "Are you ever uncomfortable with the way conflict is handled between adults in your family? If so, explain." Or, "Do you feel safe in your home? If not, explain." If clients report that violence is a part of their relationship in their individual meetings, or if they report on their intake form that they have concerns about the ways anger or conflict is handled between adults or that they feel unsafe in their homes, or if they are referred directly to our domestic violence–focused couples therapy (DVFCT) project, we ask them to complete a more extensive battery of tests. These include the Revised Conflict Tactics Scale (CTS2; Straus, Hamby, Boney-McCoy, & Sugarman, 1996) to assess for all forms of violence, the Alcohol Use Disorders Identification Test (AUDIT; Babor, Higgins-Biddle, Saunders, & Monteiro, 2001) and the Drug Abuse Screening Test—10th edition (DAST–10; Skinner, 1982) to assess for substance abuse, the Hopkins Symptom Checklist 90—Revised (SCL-90-R) to assess for depression, and the Kansas Marital Satisfaction Scale (Schumm, Nichols, Schectman, & Grigsby, 1983) to assess for relationship satisfaction.

STANDARDIZED MEASURE TO FURTHER ASSESS VIOLENCE

In addition to asking about aggression on the intake form and in the clinical interview, standardized written assessment instruments should be used. Most therapists do not use written assessment instruments. In fact, Schacht et al.'s recent research (2009) found that only about 22% of respondents used written self-report questionnaires when screening for violence, and only 7.5% of those who did use questionnaires reported using standardized, behaviorally specific questionnaires designed to measure violence.

In our program, each partner completes assessment instruments in different rooms so that they can feel safe to report on their experiences accurately and so that they will not be endangered by their responses. We use the CTS2 (Straus et al., 1996) as our primary measure of violence received and perpetrated. This scale contains 78 items and assesses severe and minor physical, psychological, and sexual violence, in addition to severe and minor injury resulting from the violence. O'Leary, Vivian, and Malone (1992) found that the use of the CTS yielded a 53% detection rate among wives in couples seeking marital therapy, compared with a rate of 6% on a written intake form and 44% with verbal questions. The CTS2 asks each partner to report the frequency and seriousness of their own abusive behavior directed toward their partner and also the frequency and seriousness of their partner's abusive behavior directed toward them. We originally conceived of our use of the CTS2 as being helpful for screening and for assessing change over time, but we soon found that completing the scale was an important way for clients to begin to examine the violence in their relationship. One female client reported, "The questions were eye openers for me. They helped me think through my problems." Another female client reported, "It caused me to evaluate the situation a little bit more than I would have otherwise. It was upsetting to do the questionnaire as I had to answer yes to questions about broken bones and bruises." We have learned that completing written assessments can be the impetus to help clients begin the hard work of making changes.

SUBSTANCE ABUSE SCREENING

We use the AUDIT (Babor et al., 2001) and the DAST–10 (Skinner, 1982) to screen for substance abuse. We admit clients scoring in Zones 1 (score of 0–7) and 2 (score of 8–15) on the AUDIT. Similarly, we admit clients scoring 2 or lower on the DAST–10, indicating either no problem or a low-level problem. The treatment recommended for people meeting these criteria on both the DAST–10 (Monitoring and Reassessment) and the AUDIT (Alcohol Education for Zone 1 and Simple Advice for Zone 2) is provided by the Substance Abuse module of our program, described later in this book, which includes information about substance abuse and a motivational interviewing–style self-assessment and goal-setting exercise. Many clients score above these cutoffs on the AUDIT and the DAST–10. Someone who has been clean for 9 months could still screen as impaired on both the DAST–10 and the AUDIT because both measures ask about use over the past year. If a potential client scores above the AUDIT cutoff or in the "Moderate" or "Substantial" levels on the DAST–10, they will be interviewed to determine the exact nature of current (i.e., past 30 days) drug or alcohol use to determine eligibility. Again, we do not use an arbitrary score on the measure to determine whether the client is eligible for treatment, but we use these tests to help initiate a discussion with both clients about their and their partner's substance use. If either partner has a serious untreated substance abuse problem or is not able to attend treatment without using, he or she would probably be referred to a substance abuse program before being accepted into our program. We also use these tests to help us determine whether the couple needs to participate in the substance abuse module, which is described more thoroughly later in this book.

DEPRESSION SCREENING

We use the Hopkins Symptom Checklist 90—Revised (SCL–90–R) Depression subscale (Derogatis & Melisaratos, 1983) to assess all potential DVFCT clients for level of depression. In a recent unpublished article (Stith, McCollum, Birkland, Ward, & Rosen, 2006), we compared men in batterer treatment who scored above the clinical cutoff on the SCL–90–R for depression with those who scored below the cutoff on depression. Participants who were depressed reported using higher levels of physical and psychological violence against their partners than did those who were not depressed. Depressed participants also reported lower levels of marital satisfaction and higher levels of anger than did nondepressed participants. However, they were not more likely to have experienced or witnessed violence as children, to be separated from partners, to be jealous, or to justify violence against wives than were those who were not depressed. Because the correlation between level of violence and depression was so high, we are concerned that co-occurring depression may lead to more severe violence. Although we do not exclude couples from treatment because of depression, we use their scores on this measure to help determine whether they need treatment for or further evaluation of their depression.

RELATIONSHIP SATISFACTION

We use the three-item Kansas Marital Satisfaction Scale (Schumm, Nichols, Schectman, & Grigsby, 1983) to assess for the level of relationship satisfaction. Clients whose relationship satisfaction is low are not excluded, but we use this score as a starting place to help us determine where clients are when they first begin treatment. As mentioned subsequently, we also interview clients to determine whether they are serious about trying to make the relationship work. We exclude clients who have already decided to divorce or end the relationship but want treatment to enhance their parenting after the divorce. We find the program's focus on strengths in the relationship is not particularly helpful with couples who are not committed to trying to make the relationship work.

INDIVIDUAL INTERVIEW AND LETHALITY ASSESSMENT

After each potential client has completed the assessment instruments, we meet with them each individually. At that time, we find out why they are interested in the program and whether they are feeling coerced into participating. Couples included in the program must participate voluntarily.

We also ask each potential participant whether they have any fear for their continued safety if they speak honestly about their concerns in front of their partner. We exclude couples if either partner fears that speaking honestly in front of the partner could endanger them. Many couples may be afraid that confronting their partner may hurt their partner's feelings or may make them angry, but most couples do not think that speaking freely will lead to their partner's violence. If a potential client indicates that she or he is afraid of the partner or if either client reports severe violence, we conduct a more thorough lethality assessment before determining the appropriate referral source.

If the client reports that violence is occurring in the relationship, before determining the appropriate treatment, we seek to assess the dangerousness and potential lethality of the situation (Holtzworth-Munroe, Beatty, & Anglin, 1995), inquiring about the severity, frequency, and chronicity of the violence; whether it has been escalating; and the victim's belief about the dangerousness of the situation. The victim's prediction of the risk of severe assault is one of the best predictors of dangerousness (Weisz, Tolman, & Saunders, 2000). However, the victim's prediction should be taken with some caution because some victims underestimate the danger they are in.

We also investigate whether guns or other weapons are available in the home; if they are, we require that all weapons be removed from the home during therapy. A variety of other factors must be considered in an initial assessment of a couple who has engaged in violence or with an individual offender or victim. Suicidality (on the part of either partner) can co-occur with partner violence, increasing its intensity. If the victim decides to end the relationship, the risk of suicidal behavior on the part of the offender can be especially high.

We also assess for psychological abuse and stalking. Although psychological abuse is generally present if physical abuse is occurring, the extent and seriousness of the abuse are indicators of the safety of the situation. Also, stalking can be an indicator of more serious physical abuse or homicide. Has the abusive partner been violent outside of the home? Have there been any arrests or protection orders in the past due to that person's violent behavior or threats of violence? If restraining or protection orders were in place, were they followed? We also seek to determine each person's history with abuse. Did they witness or experience physical abuse as a child? Do they believe that physical abuse is acceptable? Has there been violence in previous relationships? Knowing about these attitudes and experiences can help us determine appropriate treatment options. Finally, important protective factors should be assessed. Does each partner have a social support system? Does the offender appear to take responsibility for his or her actions and appear ready to make changes in his or her life? These factors interact with the risk factors described earlier in determining the acceptability of a conjoint treatment methodology.

EXCLUSION CRITERIA

After clients complete the CTS2, we compare each potential participant's responses with their partner's. At one time, we excluded couples if either partner reported receiving any acts of severe violence (e.g., choking, using a weapon, hitting with a fist). Although we continue to be concerned about severe violence, we are more concerned if there is a significant discrepancy between what one partner reports about his or her own perpetrating behavior compared with the other partner's reports of abusive behavior received from the partner. For example, if a wife reports that her husband has choked her once, hit her with a fist four times, and called her names more than six times in the past year, and the husband reports that he pushed her once in the past year, we would be concerned that the couple would probably not be appropriate for conjoint treatment. We would be concerned both that the level of violence perpetrated by the husband had been too high to safely begin treatment with a couples intervention and that the husband is not admitting to a very high level of violence. Therefore, we could not directly address the high level of violence without endangering the wife. We would be concerned that if we directly address with the husband the violence that she reported to us privately, he may become angry about her report, and she may be at risk of further violence. When clients report very high levels of violence on the CTS2 or there are serious discrepancies between husband and wife reports of violence received or perpetrated, we meet with each partner to discuss their reports. We do not tell one partner what the other partner reported, but we spend time asking them to help us understand what they reported and encourage them to tell us whether there were other incidents that they had not reported. A typical interview with a partner who reported perpetrating a small act of minor aggression when their partner reported being victimized by severe aggression might go like this:

> Therapist: I noticed on your survey you indicated that you have shoved your partner more than once last year. Can you help me understand what happened?

After the client explains what happened, the therapist might ask if the client thought their partner was afraid. The therapist might also ask the client to talk about the most recent incident when anything physical occurred. Next, the therapist might ask about the most serious incident. With the partner, the interview might go like this:

> Therapist: I noticed on your survey you indicated that your partner choked you and shoved you against the wall last year. Can you help me understand what happened?

After the client explains what happened, the therapist might ask if the client was fearful when the incident happened. The therapist would also ask whether the client thought his or her partner would mention these incidents on the survey and how the participant might think the partner would respond if the therapist talked with him or her about the incident. It would also be important to find out whether the client felt safe talking about the incident with the partner in session.

In one situation, we had a couple, "Mary" and "Bob," who came to our clinic for an assessment. Bob reported that he shoved his partner once. Mary reported ongoing severe violence, including choking, beating, and forced sex. When Mary was asked about the incident, she said, "Don't let Bob know I told you about these incidents." When asked why, Mary said, "I'm afraid he would kill me if he found out I told you about what he had done." Of course, the two of them were not considered appropriate for couples treatment. We explained privately to Mary that we felt strongly that couples treatment was dangerous in her situation. Often, couples discuss difficult issues in couples therapy, and if either person fears that being honest with the partner could lead to increased violence, couples therapy is not appropriate. We gave Mary numbers for the local battered women's shelter, worked with her to develop a safety plan (described in more depth in a later chapter), and gave her resources for individual therapy, if she decided to seek help for herself. We also told her of our plan for a joint meeting with her husband. At that time, we told both partners that we decided that they did not meet the criteria for being in our project. We said that we believed that they each had individual issues they needed to address before beginning couples treatment and encouraged them both to seek individual therapy. We gave them appropriate referrals.

In another case, both partners may report independently that the husband choked the wife. Both may also report that this incident was what led them to know they needed help. In that case, we may decide to allow them to begin treatment. If we find both partners are in agreement that a high level of severe violence has occurred, we interview each of them separately to determine whether changes have occurred that may make the home safer. For example, we have had clients with a history of severe violence participate in our program after the offender has completed a batterer program or substance abuse program. Because our program has many safety procedures and ongoing screening, we have found that using an arbitrary exclusion screening criteria is not necessary. However, in general, we exclude clients if

- either partner is fearful that the other could get violent in response to anything said in conjoint therapy.
- there is a significant discrepancy between partners in response to the CTS2, that is, if one partner reports receiving considerably more serious abuse than the other partner reports perpetrating, especially if she or he does not feel safe talking about the discrepancy.
- either partner has a serious untreated substance abuse problem or is not able to attend treatment without using. He or she would probably be referred to a substance abuse program before being accepted into our program.

- the couple is not willing to remove weapons, especially handguns, from the home during treatment.
- both partners are not willing to consider maintaining the relationships. We have found that the program described in this book does not work well with couples seeking a divorce. It could be modified to meet the needs of these types of couples, but as developed and tested, we exclude couples who choose to separate.

OTHER CONSIDERATIONS FOR ASSESSMENT

The overall assessment should be undertaken in the context of a working alliance (O'Leary & Murphy, 1999). High dropout rates among this group often come from a punitive rather than a supportive approach to assessment and treatment. Both partners often expect to be blamed. Also, any good assessment should also assess strengths and resources. Any treatment plan that comes out of this assessment should build on preexisting strengths and coping strategies.

If we decide that DVFCT is not appropriate for a particular client, we have a variety of potential referral sources. We often refer to the local domestic violence treatment providers (e.g., batterer intervention groups, victim support services, shelters). We also refer to local substance abuse services, to community mental health services, or to practitioners whom we believe would be more appropriate for a couple's issues.

3

DOMESTIC VIOLENCE–FOCUSED COUPLES THERAPY WITHIN A SOLUTION-FOCUSED FRAMEWORK

Domestic violence–focused couples therapy (DVFCT) is based on the solution-focused brief therapy (SFBT) work of de Shazer and Berg (de Shazer et al., 2007), but that model has been modified to fit the realities of domestic violence work. In short, we work with the couples with a strength and competency focus as long as we do not encounter constraints that compel us to use interventions from other models. These constraints include threats to safety, the need to deal with the painful legacy of past violence, the recurrence of violence, depression, and so forth.

To guide us, we have adopted Dan Wile's (1993) idea of primary and secondary *therapeutic pictures* in couples treatment. A therapist's *primary picture* is the set of working assumptions about people and therapy with which he or she prefers to work. This set of ideas is the framework that guides the therapist's thinking even before he or she has met the client, and it is the framework that will be abandoned only when there is sufficient evidence that it is no longer advantageous. The therapist's *secondary picture* is the set of ideas, techniques and approaches that he or she adopts when constraints arise that prevent the use of the primary picture. According to Wile, secondary pictures apply when the therapist is unable to see, in the present moment, how to apply his or her primary picture or when the immediate data suggest another approach. For instance, a couple therapist whose primary picture is cognitive–behavioral might assume that faulty cognitions and skill deficits lead couples to experience problems. Therapeutic action will involve challenging faulty ideas ("My husband should know what I want emotionally without my having to tell him") and teaching skills—in this case, communication. However, suppose during a session that a client suddenly becomes quite emotional and says that the difficulty she has talking to her husband is reminiscent of the difficulty she had feeling that her father really understood or valued her. The therapist may choose to ignore this information and proceed with skill training, but if it has sufficient intensity or persistence, it may need to be attended to. In that case, the therapist may adopt a secondary picture—in this example, perhaps the "past reflected in the present" model—as a way to deal with this bit of data from the client. Typically, the therapist will try to return to his or her preferred or primary picture as quickly as possible. Thus, a cognitive–behavioral marital therapist, faced with an outpouring of intense emotion, will adopt an empathic and expressive stance with the client as a way to deal with the emotion to the point that the session can return to the primary picture of examining faulty thinking and teaching needed skills. We have modified Wile's schema slightly to focus not on how immediate data in the session may lead us to a different therapeutic picture but rather on how constraints do so. We try to use the solution-focused picture unless we feel constrained not to do so. As we describe in more detail subsequently, the primary constraint we encounter is a situation that we believe demands a more therapist-directed stance than will fit within the solution-focused model.

SOLUTION-FOCUSED BRIEF THERAPY—THE PRIMARY PICTURE

Although detailed descriptions of this model and its assumptions exist elsewhere, the following five broad components form the theoretical foundation for our approach. These components are derived from the definition of SFBT currently being developed by the Solution-Focused Brief Therapy Association.

The Appreciative Stance

Foundational to our work with couples is the *appreciative stance*. This is our basic belief and orienting posture in interactions with clients and is based on the presupposition that clients bring not only problems but also large measures of competence, resources, and strength when they come to treatment. These areas of competence are often obscured by clients' and other service providers' focus on problems and broad labels (e.g., *batterer*, *victim*) that do not leave room for more complex understandings. Using the presupposition of strength as a lens, we then observe, ask questions, and gather data to begin to develop a picture of our clients that includes the areas of success and competence already occurring in their lives. Finally, we try to reflect this vision of our clients back to them in language that they find both familiar and believable. Although the specific techniques of SFBT (e.g., the miracle question, scaling, looking for exceptions) can be used from within a variety of theoretical approaches, we see adopting the appreciative stance as key to truly using SFBT. Without the appreciative stance, therapists will lose confidence in the search for strengths as problem descriptions and broad labels reassert themselves.

Descriptions of Solutions

In contrast to approaches that emphasize a detailed understanding and description of the problem and its interactional context, a tenet of DVFCT is that generating more complex and elaborated descriptions of the absence of the problem is useful in treatment. Often, couples' goals for treatment are appropriate but vague—for example, "We'll be happy together"; "We'll get along"—whereas their complaints are well developed and specific—for example, "When we talk about money problems, he gets mad and just walks away. If I follow him and try to make him finish the conversation he'll get madder and that's when he hits me. If I don't follow him, we never talk about it again."

Creating a specific and detailed picture of the desired outcome has several advantages. First, it gives clients a concrete picture of the goals they are working toward, allowing them to envision the intermediate steps and strategies they will need to reach that goal. Further, it allows them to observe the ways in which parts of their preferred outcome are already in existence in their lives. This not only gives clients hope, it also helps the therapist join with their existing competencies, typically a different experience for clients who interact with professionals primarily around their deficits—violence, danger to their children, and so forth. Finally, it points the way toward action. A basic tenet of solution-focused work is: "Do more of what works." Thus, if clients can be helped to see that some small pieces of success already exist, they can amplify those pieces, doing them more intentionally or more often.

Changing Static Descriptions to Fluid Descriptions

A third tenet of DVFCT is that life is a constant process of change, although our descriptions of it often remain static. Helping clients shift their static descriptions of problem states ("We're unhappy") to more fluid descriptions ("Sometimes we get along pretty well, and other times we fight") both reflects reality and creates a path to explore the areas of success and competence that exist in couples' lives. Seeing that there are already areas of solution helps clients (and therapists) have hope about change and build on existing pockets of solutions rather than feeling that solutions must be created anew.

Clients' Goals Structure Treatment

A fourth tenet of SFBT is that clients' goals for treatment remain in the forefront and structure treatment. This is particularly important with DVFCT because any number of "goals" have typically been imposed on clients by the time they come to therapy. The legal system may have imposed the goal of "managing anger" on the "perpetrator." The batterer's intervention program may have imposed the goal of "ending the use of male privilege." Finally, the victim's support group may have imposed the goal of "leaving the batterer" on the victim. None of these are bad or necessarily inappropriate goals. However, when they are experienced as imposed from the outside without the consent of the clients, they are hard to truly accept. We begin, then, by trying to determine which goals the couple themselves wants to work toward and use these to structure therapy. Because one of the inclusion criteria for DVFCT is that both partners pledge to end violence in the relationship and both want to remain together, we can work with stated goals that do not necessarily focus on violence per se.

Many Paths to a Solution

Finally, in contrast to some other approaches that prescribe a certain set of steps that must occur for clients to solve their problems, SFBT adopts a more flexible approach. In our view, there are many avenues clients can take to solve their problems, and none should be rejected out of hand because they do not fit the therapist's view of a "correct" solution. Sometimes, imposing a path to a solution is not only ineffective, it can also be harmful. Data suggest, for instance, that forcing people to "debrief" after traumatic experiences can be retraumatizing if they do not feel it will be helpful to them (Rose, Bisson, Churchill, & Wessely, 2002). In DVFCT, it is important to help clients develop and refine their own paths to a solution, based on amplifying pieces of the solution that are already present.

In summary, SFBT techniques are primarily linguistic and cognitive. They aim to use language carefully to change thinking with a resulting change in behavior. In doing so, the focus remains primarily on the present and especially the future. This is in contrast to approaches that have as their goal eliciting and resolving emotional conflicts or changing clients' understanding of their past experiences. The therapist approaches clients with the conviction that they have strengths and capacities on which to build solutions,

TREATMENT FORMAT

The treatment is offered in both multicouple and single-couple modalities. In both modalities, cotherapists provide the treatment. The treatment is conducted in two phases. In Phase 1, the therapy is primarily therapist-directed and psychoeducational in nature. Much of the work in the first phase is conducted with partners separated. In the single-couple format, this means one cotherapist meets with each partner during sessions. In the multicouple group format, this means that much of the work is done in men's and women's groups. This phase of treatment generally lasts 6 weeks. Phase 2 of treatment is mostly conjoint and client-led. The couples meet together with each session beginning and ending with a separate-gender interview with one of the cotherapists. A variety of safety interventions are emphasized throughout treatment. These interventions are described throughout the book. The schedule for the treatment varies according to the format. In general, the single-couple treatment is scheduled for 90 minutes and the multicouple treatment is scheduled for 120 minutes.

TREATMENT GOALS

The primary goal of treatment is the cessation of all forms of violence in the relationship. Although ending physical violence is, of course, essential, we believe it is also important to help clients recognize and eliminate other forms of violence in their relationship. We address ways that individuals are controlling of or psychologically violent to their partners and work to help clients eliminate all forms of violence. For some couples, DVFCT may allow partners to reconsider whether the relationship is viable. The treatment is considered effective if the couple remains together without violence or if the couple separates without a violent incident. Basic to the approach is a both–and position: Each individual is responsible for his or her own behavior, and individual behavior affects and is affected by the behavior of others. Minuchin and Nichols (1993) wrote, "What keeps people stuck is overlooking their own participation in the problems that plague them. What sets them free is seeing their own role in the patterns that bind them together" (p. 64). The notion of interdependence makes a lot of sense to us. That is, although the person who uses violence is accountable for his or her actions, interrupting repetitive patterns of behavior within the couple system that maintain abuse is viewed as a powerful tool to deal with the problem.

A secondary goal is to enhance positive affect and experience between partners. If the couple decides to remain together, we seek to help to increase positive affect and experience between the partners. As mentioned in

EXHIBIT 3.1
Summary of Domestic Violence–Focused Couples Therapy Goals

- End all forms of violence between partners.
- Gain the cooperation and commitment of both partners in making changes in their relationship.
- Assist partners to build on strengths and past successes to develop solutions to relationship problems.
- Identify and support relationship patterns that lead to cooperative resolution of conflict
- Enhance positive affect between partners.
- Assist partners in taking responsibility for their own behavior.
- Punctuate and solidify positive changes that are made.

Because the multicouple group format also uses the power of group interaction as a therapeutic factor, some additional goals are specific to it:
- Build group support for nonviolent healthy relationships.
- Use group process to provide support for healthy changes and challenges to abusive or disrespectful behavior.
- Encourage clients to learn from the wisdom of clients who are making positive changes.
- Build community support in same-gender and multicouple groups.

Chapter 1 of this volume, one strong risk factor for intimate partner violence is relationship distress. If couples remain together, helping them reduce relationship distress and improve relationship satisfaction is vital to eliminating violence in their relationships. Helping couples recognize and build on successes and what is going well in their relationships is the focus of the client-led portion of our treatment.

A third goal of the program is to increase each partner's responsibility for his or her own behavior. Throughout our treatment program, we work to help clients accept responsibility for their own behavior. Although we think systemically about the type of violence we seek to treat in this program (i.e., situational couple violence), we work to help each individual accept his or her own part in ending violence and improving the relationship. See Exhibit 3.1 for a summary of DVFCT treatment goals.

TREATMENT ASSUMPTIONS

Three assumptions guide our work. First, we believe that violence is a choice. We also believe that safety is paramount and that different treatments fit different couples.

Violence Is a Choice

Many individuals come to the program believing that their use of violence was caused by their partner's behavior or that their partner's use of violence was caused by addiction to substances or stressors in his or her life. Although stress and substance abuse are risk factors and may increase the likelihood that an individual may use violence, we believe that the decision to use violence is a choice. Individuals can choose to be violent or can choose to adopt other means to deal with stress. They can also choose to manage their substance use in such a way that it does not lead to a decision to use violence. Throughout the program, we emphasize that violence is a choice. We have treated many clients who have decided to eliminate violence from their repertoire, and we have no doubt that that it is possible to end violence.

Safety Is Paramount

The treatment program described in this book has specific components and a set agenda for the first 6 weeks, which are therapist-led. However, we emphasize that therapists have to use clinical judgment throughout the program to put safety first. Therapists should use their judgment to determine whether a session should not be conducted conjointly because of an increased risk of violence, or they may decide to change the order of the sessions to enhance safety. Nothing suggested in this book should take precedence over clinical judgment when it comes to client safety.

Different Treatments Fit Different Types of Violence

As emphasized throughout this book, DVFCT is designed for a specific group of couples experiencing intimate partner violence, that is, situationally violent couples. Individuals who are batterers or couples in which one partner lives in fear of his or her partner are not appropriate for this type of treatment.

WHAT DISTINGUISHES DVFCT FROM OTHER TYPES OF COUPLES TREATMENT?

It should become clear as you read this book is that DVFCT is not usual couples treatment. The treatment described here has a focus on ending violence, and we believe that this relatively brief intervention has been successful if it does so. A secondary aim is to increase relationship satisfaction. Many couples, at the end of this program, report that things are much better for them and that they are satisfied with their relationship. Our data suggest that relationship satisfaction, in fact, increases among our couples. However, the focus of DVFCT is limited and not designed to deal with every problem a couple may be facing. Often, couples will be able to eliminate violence and increase their satisfaction during DVFCT and then seek continued, more traditional, couples treatment after DVFCT is finished. They may explore posttraumatic stress disorder issues, chronic and entrenched relationship patterns, sexual issues, or a variety of other things. In these cases, we see DVFCT providing a safe foundation on which to base more intense psychotherapeutic work. The goal of the 18-week program is to end violence and begin to enhance couple relationships, not to address every issue that may get in the way of a couple having the relationship they want.

OVERVIEW OF THERAPIST-DIRECTED TREATMENT

We begin DVFCT with a therapist-directed approach because we believe it is important to provide initial structure when there has been a history of intimate partner violence. We are aware that allowing escalating interchanges to take place in couples therapy can lead to ongoing escalation after the session and thus increase the risk of violence. When working with couples who have a history of violence, we structure the initial sessions carefully and take a directive stance, controlling interaction when the couples are together. Consider this passage from the 1993 book *Family Healing* by Minuchin and Nichols:

> With most families I encourage dialogue between family members right from the beginning, as a way of exploring how people talk together and of exposing the structure of their relationships. In violent families, however, I discourage interaction. I tell couples that until they can have a dialogue with more light than heat, they should take turns, each talking to me without interruption. I do everything I can to slow them down and make them think. I encourage them to be specific, using concrete details as an antidote to emotionality. (p. 72)

We agree with this perspective and especially appreciate the reference to having a dialogue "with more light than heat." Therefore, we begin treatment with a structured therapist-led approach. In fact, the first six sessions of DVFCT are generally conducted with the partners separated—that is, one cotherapist meets with each person separately in the case of the single-couple model or with men and women in separate groups in the multicouple group format. During this phase, we seek to develop a relationship with each client, help each couple develop their vision of a healthy relationship, and give clients information about domestic violence and abusive behavior of all kinds—physical, emotional, and sexual. This often serves a consciousness-raising function as both partners realize the ways in which they have acted abusively toward each other. We also teach safety planning, time-out skills, and mindfulness meditation for self-soothing, and we provide a brief, motivational interviewing–type intervention for couples who report any drug or alcohol use. The time-out planning is typically taught with the partners together so that the use of time-out becomes a negotiated experience, not a unilateral one as is often the case when only men learn the technique in gender-specific treatment.

These individual (or gender-specific group) sessions also allow for continuing evaluation of the appropriateness of the couple for conjoint work. There can be considerable flexibility in this phase of treatment. Although we describe the typical sequence of content covered in the session, the sequence can be varied as needed. For instance, we might provide safety planning immediately when couples appear not to have or use such skills. Safety remains the primary concern throughout the course of DVFCT, and clinicians are encouraged to modify the sequence of structure of the sessions at any time in the interest of safety.

Although there is considerable focus on psychoeducation in the first 6 weeks of the program, we use the same solution-focused approach with these sessions as we use throughout the program. At first, integrating psychoeducational materials into a solution-focused program may seem incongruous. Solution-focused work relies on helping clients generate their own unique solutions to difficulties, with the therapist guiding the process more than the content. Thus, a solution-focused therapist asks questions designed to help a client discover unique ways that he or she might be able to control escalation in relationships. Professionally led psychoeducation, in contrast, posits that the therapist's role is to provide content to clients that they cannot produce on their own and then help clients adapt this generic content to fit their unique situation (McFarlane, 2005). To follow with our example, using this model, a therapist might teach a generic method that a client could use to control escalation and then have the client practice it in role-play in the group, in the process adapting the generic technique to fit a couple's unique situation. Although there is certainly room for sharing ideas among group members if psychoeducation occurs in a group, the therapist remains the primary source of knowledge.

In DVFCT, we take something of a middle position. We believe strongly that clients come to us with native knowledge and skills that they can use to eliminate violence and improve couple functioning. Often, these resources are obscured because neither the clients nor their treaters believe that the clients have such resources; therefore, treaters do not ask about them and clients either do not report them or see evidence of success merely as anomalies. To counter this, we try to be intentional about eliciting clients' knowledge and strengths, and we emphasize and dissect success experiences to help clients see how they have acted well on their own behalf. At the same time, when dealing with violence, there are times when we also believe we have knowledge that clients need. On occasion, for instance, clients have reported that going for a drive when they are angry and taking a time out is a strategy they would like to try. However, we believe strongly that driving while angry is not a

Week 1: Joining and Honoring the Problem (gender-specific session)
Week 2: Defining the Miracle (conjoint session)
Week 3: Introduction to Intimate Partner Violence (gender-specific session)
Week 4: Mindfulness and Safety Planning (gender-specific session)
Week 5: Negotiated Time-Out (gender-specific + conjoint session)
Week 6: Substance Abuse Module (gender-specific session)

good idea and may lead to other difficulties. When a client proposes this as a solution, we feel compelled to raise questions and provide some education about the dangers of road rage and angry driving. To reconcile this difference, we have developed a stance we call "teach last." In this stance, we seek first to elicit the clients' ideas, knowledge, and successful strategies about the evening's topic, adding the therapist's ideas or information only as a last resort when we feel that the group has not contributed vital information.

The following brief group vignette illustrates how we integrate psycho-education into an SFBT-guided program. The topic for the evening is recognizing escalation signals. In the initial stages of the session as clients are reporting their experiences since the previous session, one man talks about how irritated he becomes when his female partner accuses him of not listening. Somewhat as an aside, he mentions that he is showing more self-control in these situations than he used to in the past. In the normal course of group inter-action, this comment might go unnoticed or unacknowledged. However, one of the cotherapists stops him and says the following:

> Let me ask you about one of the other things you said; you said that you feel like you exercise more self-control. You went by that pretty quick. But that's a big thing, and that's really essentially what this first issue is about, exercising self-control, so I want to ask you a little more about that. It's one thing to say, "I've had more self-control." It's another thing to actually [exercise that self-control]—How have you done that? What sorts of things have helped you exercise more self-control thus far?

The client's description of his efforts to control his irritation when his partner accuses him of not listening provides a way for the therapist to begin the discussion of the intended topic of the session. The client's own strategies of self-control provide the basis for talking about ways to recognize and inter-rupt the escalation of arousal that can lead to increased conflict.

Refer to Exhibit 3.2 for an outline of the therapist-directed sessions in DVFCT. In Chapters 4 through 9, we describe each session in more depth and provide examples based on our clinical experience to illustrate key topics and techniques.

4

SESSION 1: HONORING THE PROBLEM

In the chapters that follow, we expand on the content and process that occur in each of the subsequent sessions. In this chapter, we discuss the procedure for the first session, which takes place after the intake screening. The format of the first session differs depending on whether it is a multicouple group or a single-couple session.

INTRODUCTIONS AND GROUND RULES

The first multicouple session begins with cotherapists and clients meeting together in the same room. The therapists welcome everyone and introduce themselves to the group. Next, everyone introduces themselves and tells the group something about themselves (e.g., how long they have lived in the area, how many children they have, their hobbies). We explain to the group members that, in our experience, couples treatment works best if therapists have a chance to work with men and women separately on their own issues before starting to meet together and address couples issues. We also explain that the group has two purposes. We want to help couples prevent the recurrence of physical and psychological aggression in their relationships. However, we also want to help them achieve more satisfaction and enjoyment together. The key to eliminating aggression and abuse is taking personal responsibility for one's actions. The key to decreasing the risk for future aggression is improving the quality of relationships.

We explain that in the next session the men and women will work together to establish goals for treatment, and the treatment program will be designed to meet the client-selected goals. We also let them know that most of the first six sessions will be conducted in men's and women's groups. The men's and women's groups will focus on a broad outline of issues to be addressed each week, such as ways to manage anger and conflict, how to relax, and so on. Clients will often be given a handout that summarizes content of the session during the first 6 weeks. Clients may have the opportunity to bring up their own issues during the first 6 weeks, but the focus will be on each person taking responsibility for his or her own behavior, not on discussing the flaws of the partner. We explain that therapists will switch groups each week so that each therapist will get to know each client and so that clients feel comfortable with all therapists.

Next, the group members will be asked to develop group ground rules. The rules provide a common understanding of how the group will operate. We begin by asking the clients to brainstorm what they think should be in the group rules. When asked by a researcher what was helpful about the first session, one male client said:

Male Client: Stating the rules at the beginning was a good idea.

Interviewer: So, that was helpful.

Male Client: Yes, that was helpful. But it wasn't, like I said, I'll rephrase that, it wasn't stating the rules, it was allowing people in the group to make the rules. That gave a lot more freedom of will. In fact, I think that was incredibly smart. Because it not only told these people, if we give you the choice to make the rules, that's also basically saying, we'll also give you the choice to say what you want. If you want to be more interactive as the group goes on, then do it at your own pace. I don't think anybody was forced to do anything they didn't want. . . . I think, for example, [another male client]. He was real nervous at first, and he started relaxing and getting more interactive as the session went on. So I think that letting people make the rules in the beginning. Very smart idea.

Although we believe that it is important for groups to make their own rules, we make sure that the rules include the following:

- Information that is shared within the group is confidential.
- All participants speak for themselves and not for their partners.

- The group begins on time.
- No one should be coerced into speaking if he or she is not comfortable.
- What is discussed in the men's and women's groups is not shared outside those groups except by the person involved. That is, if a man raises a concern about his marriage in the men's group, he is the only one who can share it in the larger couples group. Furthermore, because safety is primary, partners may not share with one another what was discussed in the men's and women's groups after they leave the group.
- No one can participate in the group under the influence of drugs or alcohol.

Group members may come up with other rules, but we believe it is important to include these. After we have discussed the format and procedure of the treatment, the men's and women's groups meet in separate rooms.

GENDER-SPECIFIC PORTION OF SESSION 1

The rest of the session will be gender-specific (i.e., men's group and women's group). Clients are complimented for their willingness to come to treatment and work on their relationships. The goal of the conversation is to engender hope and to help clients feel respected. When interviewed by a project researcher about his experience in the program, one male client talked specifically about his appreciation that the therapists complimented him on his courage for coming to therapy:

> I like the way they acknowledge right up front, they said, "I know it took a lot of courage for you to come here." I appreciate that. I like the way they acknowledge—because it does. It takes a lot to go in there and start talking to people that you don't know about something you're having a problem with.

Because the primary goals of the first session are to begin to build relationships among group members and to develop an alliance between the therapists and the clients, we devote significant time in the rest of the session to having clients tell their stories. Although the stories are generally full of pain and not focused on strengths, we believe it is important for them to know that we respect the pain they have experienced and that we are starting this work where they are. The therapists at this time use reflective listening and comment on the resilience the participants exhibit to be here to be working on this difficult challenge.

At this point, if there is time, we often find it helpful to talk about presession change. Questions about presession change are a solution-focused technique that serves a number of purposes. The format of the questions is to ask clients to think back to when they first knew that they would be coming to couples treatment. For some, this may have been a specific decision they made. Others may have acquiesced to a partner's demand they come or felt that the level of conflict in the relationship left them no choice. We often hear from couples that they see couples treatment as their last resort before divorce. Regardless of how they decided to come, we compliment them on deciding to do something to make a difference in their relationship. We then tell them that people often notice some small changes happening once they have made a decision to come to therapy and that if they have noticed any changes, we would like to hear about them. We make clear that we are not saying that all the problems have been solved, nor are we thinking the changes are enormous, but we emphasize that we want to make room for discussions of things going better when that is true.

A way to ask this question is:

> You know, therapists often forget to ask a very important question at the beginning of therapy. We have learned that many people already start to make some positive changes before they even begin therapy, but we don't find out about those changes because we forget to ask. It's certainly important for us to talk about the problems, but we'd like to end this evening's session by asking what positive changes you've noticed in yourself or your relationship since you found out that you would be coming here.

As de Shazer et al. (2007) pointed out, there are three possible responses to presession change inquiries. First, the clients may report that nothing has changed. If so, it is important not to argue but simply to go on and ask how they hope the group will be helpful. Other clients will, in fact, report that things have gotten somewhat better. They may report on a positive experience or interaction, for instance, that seemed out of the ordinary. The therapists' response to this should be to "make it bigger" by asking detailed questions about the experience—what happened, who was involved, how did it feel when things went better, and so forth. Most important, the therapists should ask what contributions the clients themselves made to things going better. It is tempting for clients to report how others are responsible for the change ("My husband didn't get in my face like he always does"), but each interaction is, in fact, an interaction, and the therapists can focus on how the client made a difference in his or her response or in what led up to it. This begins the process of taking responsibility for oneself by looking at one's own contributions to positive interactions. Knowing that we want to understand how clients help things go better can help clients feel more comfortable when we need to talk about things they need to change or ways that they contribute to the problems. Presession change questions are based on the solution-focused model's assumptions that change is always happening and that nothing is static (Weiner-Davis, de Shazer, & Gingerich, 1987). Although we recognize that change is always occurring, if therapists do not ask about change, it is often not noted by clients or therapists.

This question is not asked simply to create a catalog of changes. As the discussion continues among the group members, if any participants are able to recognize positive changes in their relationship, this can be highlighted. For example:

> You know, as I listen to you talk about all the things you've changed even before you've come here to this group, I'm very encouraged. I recognize that some of you haven't brought up any positive changes, but the fact that several of you have noted changes, lets me know that this is going to be a group in which participants are willing to work, and work hard, at making things better in their relationship. I'm going to send you all home with an assignment, between now and the next week, I'd like you to notice ways that things are getting better in your relationships, and especially, I'd like you to notice what you are doing to help create this difference. We're going to start our [men's or women's] group with your report of differences next week.

At times, no group member is able to report any presession change, and instead group members are intent on making sure the therapist understands the seriousness of the problem. Pushing them to see what has been different when they do not yet feel the therapist appreciates the gravity of their situation will likely leave them feeling misunderstood and skeptical about therapy, especially with an issue as serious as domestic violence. Rather than push clients to report about presession change, the therapist should hear some of the story of the problem before pushing for exceptions to the problem. We find it helpful to suggest that clients may need to "let off some steam" about their situation, and we wonder with them whether that would help. Then, rather than suggesting that positive things have happened, we ask them how they have coped with such a difficult predicament. This gives them a chance to tell us about strengths without us having to disqualify their view of the situation as being without positive aspects right now.

If we run out of time hearing each person's story and do not have time to ask participants to report on presession change, we end the session with an assignment to pay attention to positive aspects of their relationship and to early signs of change, and their part in the changes, then we let them know that we will begin the next session with this report.

SINGLE-COUPLE TREATMENT

Single-couple treatment proceeds in a similar way to the multicouple group. The cotherapists meet with the couple and explain the program and its format (as described earlier). The clients are asked about themselves, such as, "How long have you lived in the area?" "I noticed on the intake that you have three children. Why don't you tell me about them?" "What kind of work do you do?" We encourage therapists to be friendly and welcoming but to block any discussion of problems in the couple's relationship until the separate-gender sessions.

After the cotherapists have met with the couple together, the rest of the session is conducted individually with one therapist and one client. As in the multicouple group, the therapist compliments each person on his or her willingness to participate in couple's treatment. At this time, the therapist seeks to understand the struggles the clients face and what led them to come to therapy at this time. Finally, as in the multicouple treatment, the therapist asks about presession change, or if there is not enough time, asks the clients to pay attention to positive aspects of their relationship and to early signs of change, and their part in any changes. The clients are asked to be prepared to talk about these changes the next week.

See Exhibit 4.1 for a checklist summarizing key elements of Session 1.

EXHIBIT 4.1
Checklist of Key Elements in Domestic
Violence–Focused Couples Therapy Session 1

1. Meet with all clients and cotherapists in the same room.
   - Welcome participants and introduce cotherapists and clients.
   - Provide an overview of the treatment program.
   - Develop group rules (multicouple group only).
2. Separate-gender treatment:
   - Compliment client(s) for being willing to come to counseling.
   - Listen to clients' stories.
   - Support clients' resiliencies and abilities to cope with difficult situations.
   - Ask about presession change.
3. Homework:
   - Ask each individual to pay attention to positive aspects of his or her relationship, to early signs of change, and to his or her role in the change.
   - Let clients know that the separate-gender meeting will begin next week with a discussion of what participants have noticed.

TROUBLESHOOTING SESSION 1

As we continue to practice and refine our treatment program, we find that certain obstacles crop up as part of the normal course of interactions. Here we summarize some of the most common obstacles and offer some tips for how to work through them.

First, we have found that people minimize violence. Although this program works to amplify strengths and avoid shaming clients, it is important for each partner to recognize verbal and physical abuse and to know that they do not have to live with violence in their lives. When clients talk about receiving physically or psychologically abusive behavior from their partner but minimize it, it is often helpful for the therapist to label the behavior as violent or abusive. If the client's life was endangered, this should be pointed out. If an abusive partner minimizes the abuse, it is often helpful to make a comment such as, "Because I know how much you care about _____, it must have been very frightening to you to realize how much you hurt him or her" or "how you could have really hurt him or her." Helping clients recognize the violence occurring in their lives is a first step toward helping them end it. This work is often most effective when done in separate-gender treatment so that the partner does not feel shamed in front of the other partner.

Second, people often express a need to address pain and anger before they can deal with solutions. Some couples we work with have expressed concern when the therapist seems to be pushing too hard for signs of progress and strengths. Clients have reported that it is important that their partner recognizes the pain he or she has caused and takes ownership for it before they feel safe examining solutions and strengths. We believe that it is always important to listen to clients and to meet them where they are. Going at clients' pace and listening to them is an important aspect of the model.

Finally, clients may find it hard to accept responsibility for their own actions. It is important that clients have a chance to describe their difficulties in the first session, but it is also important the session not become simply a condemnation of their partners. Many of our clients feel aggrieved by their partner's actions and seem to have little overt ability to see their part in what has been going wrong. This creates a creative tension for therapists, who must both hear the struggle and gently direct the clients toward attending to what they have control over—namely, themselves and their own actions. We find it helpful to empathize and then to redirect the topic to what the client might do differently in the future. Without empathizing, we find that we simply encounter renewed attempts to let us know how difficult things are.

5

SESSION 2: THE FOUNDATION FOR DOMESTIC VIOLENCE–FOCUSED COUPLES THERAPY— DEFINING THE MIRACLE

After the initial steps toward joining in Session 1, the next session focuses on helping couples articulate for themselves and the therapists their vision of a preferred future—helping them develop a rich description of their lives and their relationship without violence. The relational changes that couples are challenged to make in the course of domestic violence–focused couples therapy (DVFCT) can be difficult and intense. Leaving behind the suffering associated with their problems provides some motivation to make those changes, but we also believe that a clear vision of how they would like things to be can provide important motivation as well. Knowing where you want to go makes many alternative routes available.

When we are working with a single couple, we use the solution-focused technique of the miracle question (see de Shazer et al., 2007) to begin orienting the couple to their preferred future. As we explain subsequently, we adapt this approach somewhat when working with multicouple groups, but in both settings, we help couples focus on how they would like the future to be. This is far from an academic exercise. Their vision of the future serves as the anchor for the rest of treatment. Throughout the rest of the program, clients are asked to recall the miracle they have envisioned as a source of direction and hope.

Although therapists who are unfamiliar with the use of the miracle question sometimes fear that the miracles their clients envision will be unattainable, lacking depth, or inappropriate, we have found just the opposite. Far from describing extravagant miracles, most of our client simply want to feel closer to one another, to enjoy life, and for the conflicts they struggle with to be manageable. Achieving those simple goals improves their lives in ways that do, in fact, seem miraculous.

SESSION 2 FORMAT AND PROCEDURE

Although its name suggests that the miracle question is simply a question, in fact it is a process of asking questions and making clarifications that takes a whole session and leads the clients to articulate their vision clearly. We begin by describing the general elements of the miracle question and then illustrate how we implement them in both single-couple and the multi-couple format.

The miracle question begins with asking the clients to imagine that they have gone to sleep and, while asleep, a miracle happened. The result of this miracle is that all of the difficulties that brought them to treatment have been solved. However, because they were asleep, they didn't know the miracle had happened and must instead discover its effects as they begin as normal day. Thus, clients are asked to describe what they would encounter that would tell them that things had changed. They are urged to make the description specific and behavioral to anchor it firmly. If clients respond, for instance, that they would be happy, the therapists inquire about how happiness would be evident. What would the clients see themselves doing that would tell them they were happy? What would someone else see?

The next aspect of the miracle question is to ask how the changes would be reflected in relationships. We might ask a married client, for instance, "If you were happier, what do you think your wife would see you doing differently on the morning after the miracle that would tell her you were happier?"

I might take a minute to sit and have a second cup of coffee with her in the morning instead of rushing off to work.

The therapist could then ask the client's wife, "If your husband took the time to have a second cup of coffee with you that morning, what might he see back from you?"

The client's wife might reply, "Well, I think he would see me smiling more."

The therapists continue weaving back and forth between the couple, making the miracle interactional as well as individual. Gradually, the scope of the interaction can be widened. We have found that one of the most profound questions couples can be asked is how their children would realize that a miracle had happened. This gently confronts them with the impact that their marital problems have had on their children. It is important for therapists to not rush in this process and to give clients plenty of space to elaborate the effects of their miracle.

The next step in the miracle question process is to ask the couple a scaling question. "So, on a scale of 0 to 10, where 0 is where you were the day you decided to come here for counseling and 10 is the morning after the miracle, where would you say you are today?"

The numerical scale accomplishes several ends. First, it allows for consideration of progress already made. If the clients say they are at 4, it means that they have already made some progress toward their desired outcome. Second, it allows for the consideration of exceptions—times when things have gone better than expected—about which the therapists can inquire. Exceptions provide toeholds on which more progress can be built. Finally, the scale provides for looking at a series of steps toward the miracle rather than simply focusing on the endpoint. When focusing only on the endpoint, couples can become easily overwhelmed with the discrepancy between where they are now and where they would like to be. Moving from 4 to 10 on the scale can seem like an impossible task. However, moving from 4 to 5 may seem well within reach. In fact, asking the clients whether and how they would like to move forward by a small increment on the scale is the last component of the miracle question miracle question process. We always emphasize that clients do not need to make any effort to change in the coming week if they do not want to do so. They have already done much to achieve whatever gains on the scale they report. However, if they would like to make some effort to move forward between now and the next session, we ask them to define what it is that they would try to do. We make sure to have each member of the couple focus on his or her own behavior, not on prescribing changes that the partner should make. These actions become the homework from the session.

According to de Shazer et al. (2007), the miracle question can serve four functions. First, it is a way to create goals for therapy. This is particularly important with DVFCT, in which the clients' goals guide much of the process of treatment. Second, the miracle question can set the stage for asking about exceptions—that is, times when the problem did not happen or when things went better than might have been anticipated. As they describe the miracle, clients may also describe times when bits of the miracle have already happened. This presages future therapist inquiries about exceptions. Third, asking the miracle question can give clients a chance to experience the miracle "virtually." Sometimes describing the miracle can actually have elements of experiencing it. Clients may turn their gaze away as they talk about how things would be different, as if the inner experience is quite real, almost like a mild hypnotic experience. This experience may provide a resource as clients vividly experience some sense of change or success. Finally, the miracle question begins to define therapy as a process in which the therapists are interested in successes and progress. People are socialized to approach professionals with problems, and discussion of successes may seem out of character for a professional encounter unless the therapist specifically sets the stage for it.

What we have just described is the basic format for asking the miracle question. We now describe how we use this approach in both the individual-couple and multicouple group formats of DVFCT.

Adapting the Miracle Question for Multicouple Format: The Healthy Relationship House

In the multicouple group, asking each couple the miracle question individually while the others listen can be time-consuming and also curtail the kind of group interaction that will keep all clients involved in the process. To achieve similar ends, we have adapted the miracle question to be used in the multicouple group. We use a specific group exercise called the Healthy Relationship House.

For this activity we use a version of an activity developed by the Wilder Foundation, the "House of Abuse" (Matthews, 1995). In our adaptation, we ask clients to consider a "Healthy Relationship House." We bring flip-chart paper and markers to the session and prepare to note responses on the flip chart. On the flip chart, the therapist draws the stick outline of a house with several floors and multiple rooms. Couples are then asked to describe what qualities they think would be part of a healthy couple relationship. We find that asking about the vision of a healthy relationship in the third person helps clients envision healthy relationships when they have difficulty thinking about their own relationship. Couples can be asked, "What relationship qualities would be in the rooms of this house that would make it a house someone would like to live in?" As clients describe the qualities, the therapists write the qualities on the flip chart in the rooms of the house, as shown in Figure 5.1.

Although the therapists write general labels on the flip chart, it is useful to have the couples give specific examples of the qualities as they suggest them. Expand the descriptions of specific examples to other clients to keep the group members involved. For instance:

Client: I think one of the qualities would be companionship.

Therapist: [Writes "Companionship" in a room on the flip chart] So how would companionship show up in a relationship? What would tell you a couple had companionship as part of their relationship?

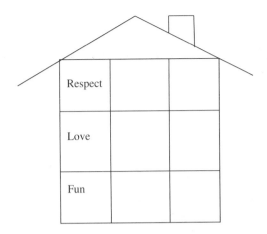

Figure 5.1. Healthy Relationship House with client-generated relationship qualities partially filled in.

> *Client:* They would do things together, things they both enjoyed, like going to a movie or taking a walk in the neighborhood.
>
> *Therapist:* [To other group members] Are there other ways that companionship would show up in a relationship?
>
> *Client 2:* Maybe they would set aside one night every week when they both promised to be at home with no outside activities . . . just them.

Encouraging Couples to Look for Parts of the Vision That Are Already Occurring

When the clients seem to have exhausted the list of qualities of a healthy relationship, it is important to sum up the vision and help group members recognize what part of that vision is already occurring. The therapists should go over the qualities listed in the diagram once more and remind the couples of how each would be enacted in a healthy relationship. Then the therapists ask each couple in turn: "Even if it is happening in only a small way, which of these qualities is already happening in your relationship?" It is important to make this an open-ended question, not a yes–no question. If the therapists ask, "Are any of these qualities happening?" it will be too easy for the clients to simply deny it. Assuming that some of the qualities are already present is important in asking the clients to elaborate.

As couples say which qualities are already there, the therapists follow with questions to make their descriptions more concrete and specific. For example, if a couple said there is some respect in their relationship: "What do you see happening that tells you that you respect each other?" or "If I had a video of you two at home, what would I see that would tell me you have respect in your relationship?"

To keep the all clients involved, as the couples answer, the therapist points out the commonalities between them:

Male Client: I think, on our good days, I have trust for Mary Ann.

Therapist: So how does that show up?

Male Client: I know she's going to do what she says she'll do with the kids, for instance. If she says they'll get to something after school, I know she'll take them.

Therapist: OK, good. That sounds a little like what Don and Angela said—that they can count on each other at least some of the time. Don, Angela, is that right?

If a couple says that none of the qualities is occurring, we greet that statement first with a short period of silence to give them time to think. If they still respond that none of the qualities is occurring, the therapist can acknowledge that this must be difficult and move on to the next couple. Therapists should not try to force couples to say something is there when they truly feel it is not.

Projecting the Vision Into the Future

At this point, we ask a version of the miracle question to help each couple personalize the relationship qualities they have generated as a group and project that vision into the future.

We want to ask you a different kind of question now. Suppose tonight when you get home, you do whatever you usually do on a typical evening and then you go to bed. You fall asleep and sleep deeply and soundly. But while you are asleep, a miracle happens, and when you awake, your relationship has all of the qualities of a good relationship that we have been talking about. However, this miraculous change happened while you were asleep, so you don't know anything has changed until you notice the effects of that change. What would be the first things to happen that would tell you that you had a new and different relationship with all these good qualities in it?

At this point, it often helps to work with each couple for a few minutes because effectively elaborating this vision requires a series of linked questions. We follow a similar line of questions as in the individual-couple condition described earlier. We start by listening to what the couples say they would notice and then ask questions to make their responses specific and behavioral. For instance, if someone says she would notice that she was happy, the therapists can ask, "What would you be doing that would indicate you were happy?" In general, it is best if clients can describe specific behavioral indicators of the miracle that are based on more of something good happening ("We'd have more respect") rather than less of something bad happening ("She wouldn't nag so much"). For instance, the initial responses may target changes the partner would make or may involve less of something rather than more of something. For example, a female client might say, "I'd know that a miracle had happened because my husband wouldn't be in such a bad mood." Therapists can move clients toward a "more of" mind-set by asking questions such as, "What would your husband being doing if he wasn't in a bad mood? What would the bad-mood energy be converted into?"

As couples' answers become more specific and behavioral, therapists can expand the scope of questions to make the miracle more interactional—that is, to help clients imagine the impact of the miracle on their interactions with one another. For instance:

> *Therapist [to Female Client]:* So, one indication of the miracle would be that you would smile more.
>
> *Female Client:* Yes.
>
> *Therapist [to Male Partner]:* If you saw her smiling more in the morning, what do you think she might see back from you?
>
> *Male Client:* I think I'd smile at her, maybe have a second cup of coffee with her before we both had to get to work.
>
> *Therapist:* So you'd take the time for a second cup of coffee?
>
> *Male Client:* Yes.
>
> *Therapist [to Female Client]:* If he smiled more and stayed around for a second cup of coffee, what would he see back from you?
>
> *Female Client:* I don't know . . . maybe I'd ask him how his day was going to go . . . if he had anything hard coming up . . . something like that.

From here, the therapists continue weaving back and forth between the partners to explore and elaborate their description of the interpersonal ramifications of the miracle of a changed relationship.

Another avenue is to extend the interpersonal effects of the miracle beyond the couple to see how it would ripple through their daily lives. Examples of questions the therapist might ask to do this include: "OK, suppose now you get to work. You don't tell anyone that this miracle has happened but maybe people there notice something is different about you? What would they notice?" and "What would a good friend notice that would tell him or her that things are different in your relationship?"

A final, and powerful, question for couples who have children is, "How would your children know that this miracle had happened? What would they see that would tell them that your relationship had changed so much?"

The group's discussion of the healthy relationship ends with each partner being asked a scaling question:

> OK. We've had a really good discussion of the qualities of healthy relationships and how they would show up in each of your relationships. Now I want to ask you a final question. Suppose we had a scale where 10 meant that your relationship had all of these qualities and 0 was where your relationship was the day you first decided to come to this group. Where would you say you are right now on that scale? You may each have different views and that's fine. We just want to get an idea of where everyone is.

Partners indicate individually where they think they are on the scale. They are then prompted to describe what, if anything, they would be willing to do to move a half step on the scale (e.g., 4 to 4.5) between now and the next session. As noted earlier, it is important to acknowledge all the efforts clients are already making and not push them to take action if they are not ready to do so.

In most cases, we end the second session by asking clients to pay attention to parts of the miracle that are occurring in their home this week, and we let them know that we will be asking about this at the beginning of the next session. If we have concerns about tension increasing among any of the couples, we end the session with brief check-ins. In the single-couple condition, each cotherapist meets with one of the partners separately to make sure that nothing that happened in the session has led to increased risk or fear of retaliation. In the multicouple group format, the couples split into men's and women's groups for a similar brief check-in. We use this time as a debrief or a way to help ensure that couples leave the session calmly.

Finally, with the multicouple group, we save the flip-chart diagram and post it each week in the room where the conjoint session will be held as a reminder of the vision the group is working toward. It can be helpful for the therapists to refer to the diagram occasionally in subsequent sessions as couples talk about their goals and successes.

By the end of the second session, all clients should feel respected and heard by the therapists. They should be able to imagine the beginning possibility, at least, of a better relationship and a clearer vision of what that relationship would look like. Clients in the multicouple group treatment modality, in addition to feeling respected and heard by each therapist, should also begin to feel connected to the group and to respect and care about group members.

One client, when asked by a researcher what was helpful about this session, reported:

> I just felt so safe, number one. So comfortable. I feel heard. I feel with information they give me back. It's something I've looked for in other counselors, because I wanted something to go home to do. Something to work on. They asked for a vision, and that made me think, OK. I've got to get my visions. They asked for us to identify concrete things—how things worked so well this week. That would be something to work on, the week, to identify these things to help us to help ourselves by learning the patterns that work for us.

Using Information From Session 2 in Future Sessions

The scaling question asked at the end of this session should be used as a gauge for change and progress throughout the rest of program. It can be asked routinely during the presession meetings. Over time, many clients come to talk in terms of the miracle. For instance, "We had a miracle day this week." The vision remains with them and helps to anchor the treatment in movement toward a desired future.

The therapists can also use the vision of a healthy relationship that the group offered as a guide for future sessions. We try to tie the psychoeducational material to the vision discussed in this session. For example,

> You said you wanted to increase trust. One of our beliefs is that if you are going to feel safe in the relationship and feel like you can trust your partner, you need to know that things won't get out of hand, or there won't be violence. We have found that using time out can be helpful to prevent things from escalating. Are you willing to discuss this technique as a way of helping you toward your goal?

TROUBLESHOOTING THE MIRACLE QUESTION

Because the miracle question is a different kind of question than therapists are typically used to asking, therapists sometimes approach it awkwardly or with little confidence that it will "work." Elsewhere (Stith et al., in press), we have written about some of the pitfalls therapists encounter in learning to use the miracle question. We recap them briefly here.

Therapist-Led Versus Client-Led Miracle Definition

At times, it can be tempting for therapists unfamiliar with the miracle question to try to influence, subtly or not so subtly, clients to develop the "right" miracle. In DVFCT, this can be a particular temptation when the client's miracle doesn't directly address issues that the therapist feels are important, such as violence or intense conflict. For instance,

Therapist: So, as the day goes on, how else would you see the miracle showing up? What else might happen?

Client: Well, we might spend some time together in the evening listening to music. We used to do that when we were first married.

Therapist: You haven't mentioned fighting yet. What about fighting? Would not fighting be one way the miracle would happen?

Client: Yeah, I guess so.

Although not fighting might, indeed, be a good sign of the miracle from the therapist's perspective, asking about it in this way suggests to clients that they are not able to answer the question adequately without the therapist's help. Thus, ownership of the miracle definition subtly shifts from the client to the therapist and, with it, the client's investment in making the miracle come true may erode as well. It is important that therapists refrain from making suggestions about the elements of the client's miracle.

Therapists often fear that clients will develop an inappropriate or unattainable miracle vision. In relationships in which there has been violence, there is often a fear that one partner's miracle will be to control or subjugate the other partner. In our experience, this has never been the case. Recall that DVFCT is not appropriate for couples in which there is an overarching agenda of domination and control by one partner over the other. Should the therapist encounter a couple in which one partner proposes such a miracle, the initial 6-week phase of treatment might be used to assess further whether DVFCT is appropriate.

At times, clients propose external miracles such as, "I'd win the lottery and have all the money I need." Should this happen, the therapists can simply begin to ask how having all the money one needs would alter relationships and proceed from there.

Awkward Phrasing of the Miracle Question

At times, perhaps because they fear clients will not answer or will find the question off-putting, therapists seem to ask the miracle question awkwardly or in a confused manner. As trainers, we have heard some of our students timidly begin the process by saying, "Let me ask you a silly question." Of course, no client will take seriously a question that the therapist defines as silly. It is also important to make sure that all the elements of the miracle question are

1. The session is conducted with all clients and cotherapists in the room.
2. Single-couple treatment:
   - Ask the miracle question.
   - Make the question interactional.
   - Ask a scaling question.
   - Focus on times when a part of the miracle has been occurring.
   - Ask the couple to decide what they would like to do in the next week to move slightly higher on the scale.
3. Multicouple treatment:
   - Draw a house with empty rooms on flip chart.
   - Ask clients to list and describe relationship characteristics of a house in which they would like to live.
   - Encourage couples to look for parts of the healthy relationship house that are occurring in their homes.
4. Homework:
   - Ask each individual to pay attention to parts of the miracle that are occurring now, to early signs of change, and to their part in the changes.
   - Let clients know that we will begin the separate-gender meeting next week with a discussion of what they noticed.

included. It can be helpful for therapists to practice asking the miracle question before using it with individual couples or in the group. If the clients do not understand what is being asked of them, it will be difficult for them to respond clearly.

Not Following Up on Details

A final error in asking the miracle question is not following up in detail on the client's answers. Although it is called the miracle *question*, it is really a process of linked questions that lead the client to a vision of the future embedded in the details of daily life, which is where change happens. Asking for behavioral detail, getting interactional aspects of the miracle, using the scaling question, and so forth all serve a purpose in the process.

See Exhibit 5.1 for a checklist summarizing key elements of Session 2.

6

SESSION 3: INTRODUCTION TO INTIMATE PARTNER VIOLENCE

Before describing the content of Session 3, we want to describe the session check-in process that will begin each subsequent session of domestic violence–focused couples therapy. The session check-in always happens with partners separated. In the case of the multicouple group, check-in occurs in men's and women's groups. In the individual format, each cotherapist meets separately with a partner. Because one of the primary purposes of the check-in is to assess for the risk or recurrence of violence, interviewing partners separately is necessary. However, the check-in also allows for the therapists to gauge progress and allows clients to begin discussing issues privately that they may not yet be ready to bring up with their partner present.

CHECK-IN

We begin the check-in process by asking each individual a question suggested to us by our colleague Luc Isebaert, "What did you do well this past week, and what is not going well yet?" This should be more than a cursory question. Help all clients pay attention to and describe times when they were

63

able to act in ways that had the potential to move them toward their miracle. We try to focus on what the client *did* well rather than on what *went* well, for two reasons. First, the outcome of most interactions is not completely in the hands of one partner. A client could act in ways that are consistent with conflict-free relating, but his or her partner may not respond in kind. Although such an action may not have a completely successful outcome—that is, it did not *go* well—the partner may have been personally successful, that is, he or she *did* well. This approach can help clients see positive steps they have made even before there are major changes in the relationships, but it is important to keep this process from turning into blame for the other partner. Because we were not privy to the interaction, we do not know whether the client is accurately describing the partner's actions, nor do we know how the partner experienced the interaction. If clients take a blaming stance, remind them that we are simply looking for positive steps and not trying to assign blame. It may take a number of weeks for relationship patterns to shift dramatically.

Another alternative is to use a scaling question during check-in. We often use the following format:

> Think of a scale from 0 to 10. Suppose that 0 is where you were as a couple when you first made the call to come to the couples program and 10 is where you would be in that Healthy Relationship House we developed in Session 2 (or after the miracle if the couple is being seen in single-couple therapy). Where would you put yourself on that scale for this week?

Regardless of which opening one uses for the check-in, the therapist should help clients amplify and articulate any positive movement while listening respectfully to reports of difficulty and struggle. If they report progress on the scale, we inquire how they managed to make progress. What did they personally contribute to that success? Were they able to deal well with difficulties during the week—for instance, not becoming angry in a situation that would have made them quite angry in the past or refraining from expressing their anger inappropriately? If they report a decrease on the scale, compliment them on coming anyway and talk about how they coped or how they decided to keep working. The goal is always to help clients identify and describe movement toward their goal while not shutting out or minimizing difficulties.

Finally, the therapists should always assess whether any acts of physical or emotional abuse occurred in the past week. Often, clients will report this information spontaneously, but if they do not, therapists must ask explicitly about it. If a client reports that conflict has escalated to physical or psychological violence, ask for clarification. We have had a number of clients talk about throwing (or their partner throwing) a remote control during an argument over television and have had clients talk about more serious ongoing violence. Our response to the report of ongoing violence depends on its lethality and on the client's report of strategies he or she was using to prevent the violence from escalating. If the client expresses any fear, or if the violence appears to be escalating or dangerous, we would immediately help the client to develop a safety plan to help him or her remain safe. In subsequent sessions when a conjoint session is planned, we may decide to continue separate-gender sessions. A more detailed discussion of this procedure is offered later in this book.

SESSION 3 FORMAT AND PROCEDURE

This session is an introduction to intimate partner violence (IPV). In this session, we build on the vision developed in the previous session and then discuss program principles, definitions and types of abuse, the cycle of violence, and anger and IPV. Even though we are presenting a significant amount of content in this session, it is important to involve the client in the discussion. If all of the content is not covered, these discussions can continue to the next session. The material is to be considered backup material. If clients are able to discuss these issues without the handouts, they do not need to be used.

This session is primarily gender-specific—that is, the men's and women's groups meet separately, and in the single-couple condition, each partner meets separately with one of the cotherapists. At the end of the session, we have the couples reunite so we can share with everyone the content covered in each group. For example:

Therapist in Men's Group:	In the men's group, we discussed program principles, types of abuse, and the cycle of violence. We didn't have time to talk about anger. What did you cover?
Therapist in Women's Group:	Sounds like we covered the same material. I was really impressed with the depth of discussion and the openness of the women to discuss some tough issues.
Therapist in Men's Group:	I hope this discussion will lead everyone to do some thinking about the behaviors we, as individuals, use that get in the way of our goal to have the relationships we want. I also hope that everyone is able to spend some time this week enjoying each other.

| Therapist in Women's Group: | That sounds like a great homework idea. Maybe everyone can share how they were able to take time with their partner having fun this week. OK? |
| Group members: | Sure. |

The same discussion could take place when the partners reunite in the single-couple treatment program.

Psychoeducation About Intimate Partner Abuse

Let clients know that you want to cover the same material with them that their partners cover in their gender-specific session. Apologize if they feel that this format does not always allow their issues to be addressed. We have designed the program to meet the vision of a healthy relationship, as discussed in the second session. We will get to their issues but may not be able to address them in any depth until we begin meeting together with both partners present.

Review Pretest Data

Talk about your review of pretest data. In the single-couple condition, be specific about what the partner you are meeting with indicated in his or her pretest. Do not report victimization reported by the partner who is not present because this might endanger him or her. In the multicouple single-gender group, make general statements about what you found from reading the pretest.

> I noted that each of you have had experiences of either physical violence (pushing, shoving, choking, etc.) or psychological violence (yelling, etc.). A primary concern in our program is ending all types of violence. Most of you indicated on the forms that your primary goal was to improve your relationships; our belief is that the violence has to end for your goal to be achieved. Does that make sense? That's why we begin our program with some pretty concrete sessions on anger management.

Another approach might be to discuss the experience the clients had completing the pretest. Many people find completing these tools and recognizing the level of violence in their relationships to be a powerful intervention in itself.

In the single-couple condition, you may want to ask your client about some of the incidents reported and how she or he was able to make a decision to end the violence and get treatment. You can applaud the decision and affirm that it must be distressing to find oneself using this level of violence against someone you love or being in such a frightening relationship. The purpose of this intervention is to make the content of the session relevant.

Define Abuse

Clarify that the goal of the program is to end all forms of abuse. Talk about the idea that abuse exists on a continuum. No one is free from all kinds of abuse. We are all in the process of working to eliminate abuse. At this point, we give clients a handout on types of abuse (see Exhibit 6.1).

After you have distributed the handout and given individuals time to think about it, ask about the types of abuse that are occurring in their families. Talk about how each of these types of abuse can have profound impact on the family. Clients are frequently surprised by the ways we define abuse. One female client told us that she never thought she was being abusive when she threw a chair at their partner. A male client spoke about how his work as a security officer required him to intimidate others and that he knew he intimidated his wife. When the therapist asked him if he also intimidated his children, he said, "no." When the therapist asked him if his children would agree with him, he spent some time thinking and then responded, "I think they would say that I do intimidate them." When the therapist asked him how he wanted it to be, he was clear that this was not the way he wanted to be perceived by his wife and children. Our experience is that for many of our clients, recognizing that their behavior could be considered abusive has been a turning point.

In the multicouple program, we use a version of an activity described in Session 2, developed by the Wilder Foundation, the House of Abuse (Matthews, 1995). In this activity, we draw a house with many rooms on a flip chart, just as we did for the Healthy Relationship House exercise in Session 2 (see the example diagram in the chapter on Session 2). We label each room with a different type of abuse (e.g., gender privilege [men shouldn't have to wash dishes; women know what's best for children], physical abuse, psychological abuse, social isolation, intimidation) and ask group members to offer examples of these types of behaviors.

After the house is drawn and after group members talk about types of abuse, we erase or cross out the physical abuse and ask participants whether this is a house where they would want to live and where they would want their child to live. This activity helps them consider how abuse is much more than physical abuse and how creating a healthy home environment means eliminating more than physical abuse. It also contrasts with the qualities of a healthy relationship that the group developed in Session 2. You can ask the group to remember the qualities of a healthy relationship and ask whether those qualities can coexist in a house filled with the types of abuse in the current diagram. In both single-couple and multicouple groups, therapists help clients take responsibility for their abusive behavior.

EXHIBIT 6.1
Handout on Types of Abuse

Physical
The use of physical force against your partner. Examples: pushing, grabbing, hitting, punching, restraining, slapping, scratching, kicking, biting, choking, holding a hand over his or her mouth, spitting, pulling hair, throwing objects, using weapons, throwing partner against the wall, ripping clothing.

Emotional–Psychological
An attempt to make your partner feel bad about himself or herself or to attack his or her self-esteem. Examples: put-downs, insults, name-calling, playing mind games, cursing, criticism, blaming, ignoring feelings, withholding approval, humiliation, threats, isolating partner, destroying partner's things, refusing to share money, abusing pets, jealousy.

Sexual
Any forced sexual activity. Examples: physically forcing sexual intercourse, forcing sexual activity with others or objects, grabbing or mutilating genitals, nonconsensual sex, giving drugs or alcohol to force sex, photographing or videotaping sex without consent, put-downs and degrading sexual statements, withholding sex unless the partner does what you want, forcing "makeup" sex after abuse, objectifying person as a sexual object, criticizing sexual performance, unwanted touch.

Verbal
Anything said or threatened to control partner or hurt him or her emotionally. Examples: name-calling, insults, yelling, raising voice, threatening, blaming, put-downs, silent treatment.

Intimidation
Use of actions, gestures, or looks that frighten, scare, or bully a person. Past use of physical abuse increases the impact of intimidation. Intimidation is usually nonverbal. Examples: body language, getting in partner's face, standing over partner, making a fist or imitating physical abuse, clinching fists, stomping, staring, tone of voice, silent treatment, destruction of property, punching holes in walls, breaking furniture, throwing things, leaving threatening notes, hurting animals, driving dangerously.

Gender Privilege
Prerogatives one has because of one's gender; assumes that one sex is better than the other and his or her needs are more important. Examples include inappropriate generalizations (i.e., men are stronger, women need to be taken care of; men are more logical, women more emotional; men are smarter, women aren't good with numbers; men should control the finances, women aren't good with money; men aren't good with children, mothers should make all decisions about children). Limiting a partner's roles in the family because of his or her gender can be a form of abuse.

Social Isolation
Any attempt to control who a partner will see, what he or she does, or what he or she thinks or feels. Examples: keeping partner from family or friends, not allowing a partner have social contacts, limiting contact with others, limiting phone calls, taking away keys, taking away money, forbidding the partner from doing something, intercepting messages, making friends or family uncomfortable when they come over, listening to phone conversation or reading e-mail, giving partner the third degree, stalking.

EXHIBIT 6.1
Handout on Types of Abuse   *(Continued)*

Religion

Using religion as a way to control your partner. Examples: making partner attend to religious beliefs, threatening God will punish your partner, threatening damnation, making a partner participate in religious rituals, using the religious doctrine to manipulate a partner's behavior, not letting a partner participate in religious activities.

Child Abuse

Any form of abuse toward children in an attempt to control partner's behavior. Examples: threatening that the partner will not see children if he or she leaves the relationship, threatening to abuse a child if the partner does not comply with one's wishes, withholding visitation between child and partner, abusing a child because of a partner's actions.

Discuss Program Principles

We give clients (both single-couple and multicouple groups) a handout (Exhibit 6.2) that lists the program principles, and we discuss them. We clarify that these principles are often brought up again and again in our treatment. When a partner tries to justify throwing the remote control at his wife "because she kept talking during the game," we remind participants of the principle that they are 100% responsible for their own behavior.

After we talk with clients about our program principles, we ask them, "What effect does violence have on the relationship?" We let clients answer, but if appropriate, we talk with them about what we have found, that is, that violence changes everything. For example, we talk about how difficult it is to maintain respect, honesty, trust and support, intimacy, and a feeling of safety in relationships when violence occurs.

We also talk about how clients would know if the violence is self-defense or retaliation. The definition of self-defense is "minimum amount of force necessary to escape the threat." Typically, men are larger and stronger than women and are not fearful of women, but women are fearful of men. However, because the goal of our program is to end all violence, we try to make it clear that it is not justified for women to use force either. We talk with clients about the difference between self-defense and retaliation. This is a sensitive topic. We may or may not talk about self-defense, depending on the client(s).

Illustrate How Violence and Anger Work

The concept of a *cycle of violence* was originally developed by Lenore Walker in her 1979 book, *The Battered Woman*. She interviewed battered women and asked them to talk about the violence in their homes. Walker found that in most cases a pattern was present. In our work with couples, we have found it helpful to present this model. In the first phase of the model

EXHIBIT 6.2
Program Principles and Tips for Discussion

1. Every situation has better choices and worse choices. In our view, violence is a worse choice in all but the most extreme situations. We can learn to make better choices.

   Confirm that we have seen people make dramatic changes in the way they treat their partners. It's not easy to make these kinds of changes, but we have seen it happen many times.

2. Acting violently in relationships is learned in what we see in our families growing up and in what we observe in our culture—movies, popular songs, TV shows. We can change what we have learned.

   Ask about how family members handle conflict and about the impact on their children (if appropriate) of conflict and violence in their relationship. Talk about television and other media violence.

3. Sometimes violence helps us get what we want, but the cost to our relationships is high. We can learn nonviolent ways to get what we want and ways to accept the situation when we cannot.

   Ask about possible positive and negative consequences of violence. If appropriate, ask client (or group members) about positive and negative consequences to violence they have experienced.

4. Violence often occurs in a climate of blame with the belief that someone or something made us be violent. We are 100% responsible for what we do. No one controls our arms, legs, hands, and mouths but us.

   Ask participants to talk about times they have been able to control themselves and what went into them being able to do so.

5. By learning to make wiser, nonviolent choices, we can improve the quality of our lives and our relationships and help our children grow up free of fear.

   Ask participants whether they want their children to grow up in a climate of fear. Ask if they want them to learn that violence is a normal part of adult relationships.

(*escalation*), couples often notice that tension is building in the relationship. They talk about "walking on eggshells" or trying to keep things calm because they know that anger is building. Usually, the stressors (e.g., worrying over finances, conflict over children) are not put into words but are held inside, where they tend to be magnified. Communication and kindness, which may characterize the relationship at its best, diminish as the partners tend to withdraw sullenly from each other. We have found that helping couples become more aware of their rising anger (physiological changes, cognitive processes, and specific behavior) can help them take corrective action before inevitably moving to the next stage, *explosion*.

Typically, the first phase leads to an abusive episode (explosion) in which the mounting tension is explosively discharged. We help couples recognize triggers that come before the explosive incident. We have found that when couples are aware of the escalation process and the triggers, they are often able to take steps, such as a time out, which we discuss in a later chapter, to avoid reaching this stage in the cycle.

In most cases, immediately following the explosive episode comes a period of relative calm (*honeymoon*). The tension has dissipated. The more violent partner may experience remorse. Apologies, promises that the violence will not occur again, and gifts are common. Often, the more violent partner is afraid of losing his or her partner by having lost control. Many couples talk about experiencing a level of intimacy in this phase that is more intense than at any other times. The more violent partner may disclose vulnerability and intense need for his or her partner. While in the escalation stage, or immediately after the violent incident, couples may recognize that they need help. It is not uncommon during the honeymoon stage for couples to believe that their problem is solved and that the violence will not occur again. They may be resistant to developing a safety plan because they are confident that violence will not recur. However, we find that in homes experiencing chronic abuse, the honeymoon period is inevitably followed by the escalation phase.

Couples we have worked with have found the idea of a cycle helpful. We give them a copy of the handout, "The Cycle of Violence," shown in Figure 6.1, and ask them whether they have seen this type of cycle operating in

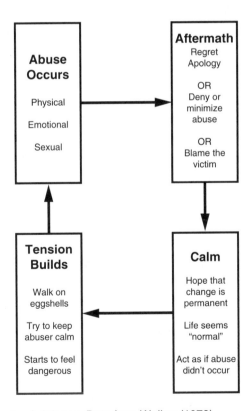

Figure 6.1. The cycle of violence. Data from Walker (1979).

EXHIBIT 6.3
Reactions to Anger

When I'm angry:	Often do this	Sometimes do this	Never do this	Comments
1. I pretend that everything is fine.				
2. I yell or lose my temper.				
3. I get sarcastic.				
4. I tell the person directly.				
5. I take it out on someone.				
6. I fight physically.				
7. I don't know until hours later.				
8. I break things.				
9. I withdraw.				
10. I'm afraid I'll hurt someone verbally.				
11. I'm afraid I'll hurt someone physically.				
12. I'm afraid I'll hurt myself.				
13. I cry.				
14. I hold it in, then explode.				
15. I express it and let go of it.				
16.				
17.				
18.				
19.				

their relationship. We ask them to talk about signs that their level of anger is escalating and also about times when they notice the escalation occurring but are able to do something different to avoid the explosion. Much of the work in the first 6 weeks of the program is designed to help them stop the escalation early in the cycle and prevent the violence from occurring.

In the final part of this session, we talk about anger and how we express it. A good resource for helping clients learn about anger is *Feeling Good, the New Mood Therapy* by David Burns (1999). We discuss how anger is typically a secondary emotion and that we have found it important to identify and deal with the primary emotion (i.e., sometimes it's easier to be angry than sad). We emphasize that your partner does not make you angry; it is the meaning you attach to his or her behavior that determines your response. We talk with clients about how our perceptions affect our level of anger (e.g., if you believe your partner was late because he does not care about you, you are more likely to be angry than if you attribute his lateness to traffic or other factors not in his control). A primary message we try to deliver in this session is that when you handle your anger well, you will have more peace and joy in your life. Finally,

EXHIBIT 6.4
Checklist of Key Elements in Domestic
Violence–Focused Couples Therapy Session 3

1. Session begins with separate-gender meetings.
2. Check-in:
   - Assess risk that may need immediate management.
   - "What have you done well since we last met, and what is not going well yet?"
   - "What parts of the miracle (individual format) or House of a Healthy Relationship (group format) did you notice during the past week?"
3. Present material on intimate partner violence in psychoeducational format:
   - Define abuse.
   - Discuss program principles.
   - Discuss connection between anger and violence.
   - Throughout, help clients apply the material covered to their specific situation.
4. Homework
   - Ask the clients to complete the "Reactions to Anger Worksheet" for the next session.
5. Session ends with partners meeting together to review the content presented.

we ask clients to complete the activity "Reactions to Anger" (Exhibit 6.3) as homework. We discuss this activity during the next session.

Finally, as mentioned earlier, we end the session by reuniting the partners (or men's and women's groups) and reviewing the material covered. If appropriate, we encourage therapists to share with clients that they were impressed with how much commitment, love, or caring was heard from members of each group. Ask them to pay attention to the way they are able to deal successfully with issues that might normally make them angry. Ask them, if appropriate, to take time this week to meet privately with their partner and to thank him or her for the willingness to embark on this effort together. For a summary of Session 3, see Exhibit 6.4.

7

SESSION 4: MINDFULNESS AND SAFETY PLANNING

If treatment proceeds in a typical sequence, this session represents the first time that we teach clients skills for dealing directly with violent actions or intense and difficult interactions. Remember that the order of the first six sessions can be changed at any time, and sometimes, if we judge that safety is a more critical issue at the time of assessment, we may start with some of the content in this session and in Session 5. Most often, however, we find that couples are more responsive to looking at skills designed to help them calm down, interrupt difficult or dangerous interactions, and ensure their own and their family's safety if we have taken the time to join with them, hear their story, and have together built a vision of the future that they wish to pursue.

SESSION 4 FORMAT AND PROCEDURE

Session 4 has two parts. First, we teach clients to use a form of mindfulness meditation to assist them in self-soothing and in becoming more aware of their physiological, emotional, and cognitive experiences so that they can identify escalation signals more readily and earlier in the escalation process.

Teaching meditation also sets the stage for the use of this technique at the beginning of each session throughout the rest of the program.

After teaching and practicing the meditation technique, we spend the rest of the session working with the clients to ensure that they have concrete plans for keeping themselves and their family members safe. Both of these components of the program—meditation and safety planning—as well as the negotiated time-out procedure that we teach in Session 5, help to form a foundation of safety-maintaining skills that will support the discussion of difficult relationship issues that occurs in the last 12 sessions of the program.

As in the preceding session, the work of Session 4 occurs in separate-gender sessions. At the end of each of these sessions, if there is time, it is a good idea to bring the groups together to summarize briefly what happened in each group. We typically summarize the information that was presented and general themes from the discussion rather than reporting specific issues raised by individuals. In taking this approach, we hope to both communicate what has happened in the individual sessions (or separate gender groups) while preserving those sessions as a safe place to talk about difficult issues that the clients may not be ready to bring up in a conjoint session. A general summary is especially important in Sessions 4 when we use different procedures to help men and women to develop a safety plan, and we do not reveal the elements of anyone's specific plan. Typically, we simply label the experience as safety planning for each group.

MEDITATION

One of the more recent additions to our model has been a component of mindfulness meditation. Mindfulness and other meditation skills have been applied to a variety of mental health problems since the early 1990s, led by the development of mindfulness-based stress reduction by Kabat-Zinn and colleagues (Kabat-Zinn, 1990; for a meta-analytic review of outcome studies, see Grossman, Niemann, Schmidt, & Walach, 2004). Baer (2003) reviewed the literature on mindfulness-based approaches and concluded that at least preliminary evidence exists for their usefulness with pain, stress, anxiety, relapse following major depression, and disordered eating. Marlatt and colleagues (for recent work on this approach, see Witkiewitz, Marlatt, & Walker, 2005) have an extensive record of research on the effectiveness of mindfulness meditation in preventing relapse in substance abuse treatment. Of most interest to us, however, was the emerging use of mindfulness meditation courses in jails and prisons, and the reductions in violence (as well as recidivism) reported as a result. Some of this early work occurred in India. In the United States, Marlatt and colleagues have been investigating the effectiveness of a 10-day Vipassana meditation course on substance abuse and other social outcomes (e.g., violence) within a U.S. prison population (Parks et al., 2003). Preliminary findings indicate reductions in drug use, problems associated with drug use, and psychiatric symptoms. In addition, meditation participants showed more optimism and internal drinking-related locus of control than those in the control group (Bowen et al., 2006).

In addition to the studies indicating that criminal behavior may decrease as a result of a mindfulness meditation course, we had other reasons to include a meditation component in domestic violence–focused couples therapy (DVFCT). One of the key interventions in our model that is designed to increase safety is the use of the time-out procedure (see Chapter 8). Before clients are able to use time outs effectively, they must be able to identify signs of increasing emotional intensity and behavioral escalation early in the cycle so that thoughtful action can be taken. When we would discuss the cycle of violence in the preceding session and asked clients to practice the time-out process, however, we discovered that many of them appeared unable to identify early signs of escalation and reported the subjective experience of going from perfect calm to intense anger or aggression in an instant. Although we remained convinced that there were intermediate steps that could be identified, our clients reported that they were unable to do so. We felt that mindfulness practice— with its focus on body sensations, thoughts, and emotions—would offer one way to sensitize clients to their emotional experience and help them know earlier in the escalation sequence when they have begun to enter a potentially abusive interactional cycle. This is similar to the case also made by Fruzzetti and Levensky (2000) in their description of the application of dialectical behavior therapy to the treatment of intimate partner violence.

We had also noticed that the time-out process itself could have an escalating effect when partners used the separation to ruminate about the interaction they had just left or about old hurts and conflicts. Although time out gave the couple a tool to separate physically before either became violent, we realized that we had not given them tools to calm and soothe themselves while apart. One clearly demonstrated effect of meditation is physiological calming and stress reduction (Kabat-Zinn, 1990), and we hypothesized that a meditation component, if used during time outs, could lead to lower physiological arousal and increased self-soothing. In fact, Siegel (2007) pointed out that the effects typically associated with a mindful state are also the effects associated with secure attachment—physiological regulation, emotional balance, attunement to others, fear modulation, response flexibility, and increased insight and empathy. Thus, we hypothesized that meditation may provide some attachment-like soothing at times of intense relationship distress.

Finally, we were also aware that many of our clients were moved to act on their internal experiences (fear, anger, hurt) almost automatically, with no consideration of the consequences of their actions. They seemed unable to step back for a moment to assess the veracity of their assumptions and reactions (e.g., "She's late . . . she must be having an affair") or to stop actions that were likely to lead to more conflict (e.g., physically pursuing or restraining a partner who was trying to take a time out). Mindfulness meditation asks clients to step out of "automatic pilot" mode and learn to observe their thoughts and impulses rather than act on them (Segal, Williams, & Teasdale, 2002). During mindfulness practice, the client is asked to notice when thoughts or other internal experiences arise and take the focus away from the object of concentration (in our case, a phrase of the client's choosing that represents a kind of secular mantra—see the meditation instructions later in the chapter). Instead of becoming further involved with the flow of thoughts, or the "story," the client notices the distraction and lets the thought go, returning the focus to the mantra. In this process, the perceived literalness of thoughts begins to loosen. Shapiro, Carlson, Astin, and Freedman (2006) described this process as *reperceiving*—that is, clients begin to disidentify with thoughts and emotions, realizing that thoughts and emotions are simply thoughts and emotions, not literal truths, and that acting on them is optional rather than automatic. Many times, acting on thoughts makes perfect sense, but sometimes it does not. Helping clients not only to understand but also to experience this distinction is a third goal of including meditation in our treatment program.

We chose to teach our clients a concentration-based approach to meditation and further chose to use a mantra (i.e., a verbal phrase repeated silently to oneself) as the focus of concentration. The other typical focus in concentration-based meditations is the sensation of breathing. We chose the mantra-based approach because it is easily taught even by relatively inexperienced therapists and because at least one approach to using it at least has been standardized for research purposes. Carrington (1998) has developed *clinically standardized meditation* specifically for use with psychotherapy clients, and it has been widely used for both clinical and research purposes (for a summary, see Carrington, 1998). In addition to its teachability and specificity, we also felt that the use of a word or phrase that the clients chose left control of the process more in their hands and provided a stronger stimulus than having them attend to the breath—another common anchor for concentration meditations. Focus on the breath can initially be more frustrating for clients, and we wanted to provide them an accessible approach. Thus, we adapted Carrington's instructions for our clients.

After the check-in, therapists begin Session 4 by teaching meditation. The following materials serve as a guide for this part of the session and are also given to the client as a handout (Exhibit 7.1). The key points are to motivate the clients to try meditation and to answer any questions or objections.

EXHIBIT 7.1
Handout on Meditation

Why meditate?

Meditation helps to calm both the body and the mind. We feel this is important for couples who are struggling with conflict because tension in a relationship often results in physical and emotional stress, which leads to more relationship conflict, which leads to more physical and emotional tension, and on and on. Research indicates that meditation has effects on both the physical and emotional effects of stress, leading to better emotional balance and better physical health. We also feel that meditation can help couples interrupt the cycle of couple conflict and personal stress that brings them to counseling.

How much do I have to meditate?

That answer will depend on you and how useful you find meditation. We suggest you start by meditating for 10 minutes twice a day—morning and afternoon/evening. We also suggest that you meditate for at least 10 minutes whenever you and your partner take a time-out to control conflict. Finally, we suggest that you meditate with your therapist briefly at the beginning of each therapy session. We would like you to try your best to stick to this schedule for the first 3 weeks of the program so that you give meditation a fair try. After that, you can work with your therapist to modify that schedule if it doesn't work for you. You will have a chance to discuss any difficulties that arise in meditation with your therapist so that you can find the best way for you to use this technique.

Isn't meditation some kind of a religion?

We are not teaching meditation as a religious practice but as a way to achieve physical and emotional balance. Of course, most religions have a meditative or contemplative component. In Christianity, for instance, this is called "centering prayer." If including your faith in your meditation seems like something that will be helpful, you can pick a meditation word or phrase that symbolizes your faith. You will have complete control over which phrase you choose and will not even be asked to tell your partner or therapist what phrase you are using unless you want to do so. You can also choose a word or phrase that is not connected to a religious tradition but that has meaning for you. We will discuss meditation phrases in a minute.

How do I meditate?

The instructions for meditation as we are teaching it are relatively simple.

Find a quiet place and sit with your eyes closed. It is best to sit up straight in a chair with both feet on the floor and your hands resting either on your legs or in your lap. However, if you find this uncomfortable for some reason, adjust your posture so you are comfortable. It is possible to meditate lying down but you will likely go to sleep, especially when you are new to meditation, so be sure to set an alarm or meditate when sleeping for a while won't interfere with other activities.

After you find a comfortable posture, take a moment just to settle and see if you can simply sense how your body feels. Any feeling is OK—the point is to be aware of what you are feeling. If you are meditating during a time-out, you may feel nervous, frustrated, tense, or any number of other unpleasant feelings. Just notice these feelings; don't try to change or control them.

After you have settled for a moment and observed how your body feels, begin to say your meditation word or phrase silently to yourself. You do not need to say it out loud. Just repeat it silently to yourself at whatever pace seems best. Sometimes you will find yourself saying the word over and over again really quickly, and other times you will say it slowly and even find yourself pausing between repetitions. There is

(continues)

EXHIBIT 7.1
Handout on Meditation   *(Continued)*

not one right way to do this meditation. Just say the word or phrase to yourself in whatever way fits at the moment.

As you repeat your phrase to yourself, you will soon find that you are distracted and are no longer paying attention to the phrase. This is entirely normal and expected. You are learning to focus your mind, and this will take time. When you realize that you are no longer focusing on your phrase or that you have stopped saying it to yourself, gently bring your attention back to the phrase. Try not to force your attention. Be patient with yourself. The process of meditation is simply to pick something to focus on, to notice when you move away from that focus, and then to bring yourself back.

At the end of your meditation period, open your eyes slowly and look around. Move your hands and legs a little bit at first. Don't jump right up and go back to activity. Give yourself a minute or two to ease out of the meditative state.

How do I time my meditation periods?

A timer with a quiet chime or beep will be most useful. Many digital watches have a timer that will beep after a set amount of time. You can also use a kitchen timer, but if it ticks or has a loud ring, put it in another room while you meditate so you can't hear it ticking and the ring can be heard but won't startle you too much. If you want to meditate and don't have a timer handy, you can open your eyes and glance at a clock or watch periodically, but this makes it hard to maintain your focus.

What word or phrase should I use to meditate?

This is entirely up to you. In some ways, the words don't make a difference. They simply give the mind something to focus on to achieve calm. You can use a nonsense syllable if you like. For instance, you might use something like "ALM," which has a nice resonant sound. Or "OME." Or "IMA." The possibilities are endless. If you are using a nonsense word, try to find one with one or two syllables. A short sound seems to work better than an extended phrase. Although nonsense syllables are fine and work well, many people like a word or phrase that has meaning to them. As with nonsense sounds, try to pick something short—just a few syllables—and easy to remember. If your religious faith is a source of comfort for you, you might pick a word or short phrase that symbolizes your faith. If you prefer a nonreligious word or phrase, here are examples of things that people have found helpful:

- LET GO
- PEACE
- CALM
- RELAX
- LET IT BE
- SLOW DOWN

Don't spend too much time trying to find the perfect phrase. As you meditate, the phrase will begin to lose its meaning and become simply a way of focusing your mind.

What do people experience during meditation?

People have all kinds of experiences while meditating. All of them are fine. Unpleasant experiences while meditating are rare. If you have any kind of very unpleasant experience, open your eyes. Usually, opening your eyes will change the experience significantly. If the experience wasn't too bad, try to continue meditating with your eyes open for the rest of the period. However, *don't ever force yourself to keep meditating if doing so makes you feel really upset, scared, or anxious.* Stop meditating. Go for a walk, talk to someone, listen to music, or do other things that

EXHIBIT 7.1
Handout on Meditation   *(Continued)*

will soothe you. Be sure to talk to your therapist about the experience during your next session.

There are some common experiences people have during meditation. Many people experience physical sensations like slight pains, twitches, or itches. At other times, people experience a sense of general restlessness, an inability to keep focused on the meditation phrase, physical restlessness, and a wish to stop meditating. Usually, these are signs that emotional "knots" are untying and the tension in them is being released. Paradoxically, this can be a sign that you are meditating more deeply than when you have a calm and peaceful meditation period, although both experiences are fine and common. Try to finish your meditation period, but remember, meditation is not torture. If you can't finish, stop and resume at your next scheduled time. The benefits of meditation don't come from forcing yourself to do unpleasant things. Sometimes people experience lightness or heaviness in their arms or legs while meditating. Others feel like they are floating or seeing themselves from above. These experiences usually indicate a deepening of concentration. If they happen, just notice them but don't become too wrapped up in them. They will come and go on their own as your level of concentration changes.

In general, there are four signs of deepening relaxation: tingling or warm feelings on the skin; parts of the body, especially hands, arms, and legs, feeling heavier; becoming more aware of minor aches and pains; and the breath changing (it may become more erratic with shallow breaths followed by deep ones or it may become light and delicate, almost disappearing). All of these things are signs of relaxation and stress release, but even if none of them happen during a meditation period, you are still benefiting.

What can I expect from meditation?
Meditation is sort of like physical exercise. You have to do it every day, and it may take a while to see and feel the effects. Don't judge the effectiveness of meditation based on your meditation sessions alone. You can have restless sessions, calm and peaceful sessions, or "blah" sessions where nothing seems to happen, just like some workouts at the gym are really invigorating, some are really tiring, and some are just boring. However, you are benefiting from each of your workouts just like you are benefiting from each of your meditation periods.

Recap: Brief Meditation Instructions
1. Sit comfortably with your back straight, if possible, your feet flat on the floor, and your hands either on your knees or thighs or held loosely in your lap.
2. Take a moment to sense the physical sensations in the body. If you feel tension in any part of the body, see whether you can relax that part, but don't worry if you can't. Just notice it.
3. Begin to say your meditation phrase quietly to yourself. Let the words go at whatever pace and rhythm seems right.
4. When you find your mind wandering from the meditation phrase to thoughts or body sensations or outside sounds or whatever, gently and patiently bring your attention back to the meditation phrase. Don't blame yourself or feel you are failing if this happens. Even people who have been meditating for years get lost in thoughts from time to time.

At the end of your meditation period, it helps to sit quietly with your eyes open for a moment before getting up and going back to regular activity. Ease your transition from meditation to activity.

TROUBLESHOOTING MEDITATION

Mindfulness meditation may be new to many of your clients. In this section, we discuss some of the issues we have faced and offer tips for working through them.

Clients may report that they are too distracted or agitated to meditate. Do not force anyone to meditate or to meditate longer than he or she wants to. Encourage clients to try the meditation even if they are agitated. Tell them that this is common and that meditating regularly can help with the agitation and restlessness. Do not force it, however. We are trying to introduce a technique that we hope the clients will find helpful, but we do not want to force them to do something they do not want to do.

Some clients report that they have lots of thoughts or other distractions and cannot focus on the mantra during much of the meditation period. Again, this is common. Everyone, even experienced meditators, goes through this experience periodically. Some of the clients' worry may come from thinking that meditation should only result in a serene or blissful state. Meditation is about learning to see what is really going on regardless of what it is. Remind the client that there is no right or wrong outcome from a meditation session and to try to pay attention to whatever arises.

Some clients may feel that meditating is against their own religious or spiritual beliefs. The handout contains a section on this issue, but if the client is convinced that the type of meditation we are teaching will violate their beliefs, do not continue. Ask instead what part of clients' religious tradition they might use in place of meditation to help calm and focus themselves on a regular basis and during time outs.

Some clients may report a disturbing experience during meditation— either in the session or during the week. If the experience is only mildly disturbing, suggest that they try meditating again if they are willing to do so, but with their eyes open or partly open. This tends to reduce the intensity of the experience. If they are reluctant to try again, do not coerce them into doing so. If the experience was really disturbing or had elements of flashbacks, ask the client to discontinue the meditation practice until you can consult with an experienced meditator or read more on the topic (see the Suggested Readings section for a list of additional resources).

SAFETY PLANNING

As noted earlier, before we move to conjoint sessions in which difficult material is bound to be discussed, we teach a number of skills to promote safety and gain control of volatile situations. One cornerstone of safety in abusive relationships is for each partner to have a clear and specific safety plan

(Jordan, Nietzel, Walker, & Logan, 2004). Comprehensive safety planning encompasses three phases: identification that risk of danger is increasing, identification of specific steps to take when recognizing danger cues, and methods of staying safe when departing from the potentially dangerous situation. Although we work with each client in this session to develop a safety plan, we recognize that the plan will need to be revisited if violence recurs or if a client is fearful at the end of any particular session. We discussed the signs of escalation in the previous session, but we expand on this during this and the next session. The primary focus of the plan we develop with clients is to determine steps to take when they sense that escalation is occurring and to develop procedures to keep themselves safe if they need to depart from a potentially dangerous situation. The remainder of Session 4 is used to help clients develop such a plan. The safety planning procedure we use may be unique for each partner, especially if there is a clear primary aggressor. In cases of bidirectional violence, there is more overlap as both partners need to plan for both aspects of safety—preventing oneself from being abusive and protecting oneself and any other family members if one's partner becomes abusive.

The purpose of the safety plan is twofold. In separate-gender sessions, both partners (and group members) develop a list of strategies they can use to keep themselves calm and in control to prevent violence. If the partner is also violent, the plan would include ways to keep each partner and the children safe if the partner becomes violent. The second aspect of the safety plan is especially important if the violence received from the partner (or the threat of violence) has been severe. In this scenario, participants will develop a plan for themselves, which they keep confidential, that they can implement in case of the threat of violence to keep themselves (and their children) safe.

Before asking participants to consider developing a safety plan, we explain that when we begin the conjoint portion of the treatment, we will be discussing heated issues and that the potential for violence to escalate is always present. Therefore, we want to make sure that clients have developed strategies to remain calm and safe. Have clients brainstorm ideas about developing a safety plan for themselves. We use the session as a way to brainstorm ideas. Here are some of the suggestions for enhancing safety that are general for both partners:

- Try not to argue in the kitchen (too many potential weapons), in the bathroom (too small, no place to go), or the bedroom (the bedroom should be a place of peace and respite). If an argument occurs, move to a neutral room.
- Take a time out or break from each other.
- Know your signs that you are getting angry and do something to manage your anger (e.g., time out, deep breathing) before you become abusive.
- Remove all weapons from the home.

- Keep children safe.
- Call 911.

We ask individuals who appear to be primarily victims of violence to develop a more detailed plan (for a sample detailed plan, see Exhibit 7.2). We ask all members of the women's group to develop a detailed plan. If a man is fearful of his safety, or if we are fearful for him, we work with him individually to develop the more detailed plan. It may be unnecessary to implement this plan, but it is important for participants who have been victims of violence to have one, just in case. Help each participant develop his or her own plan. In the group, female clients who are willing to share their plans with group members should be encouraged to do so. Other group members can offer feedback. We document in each participant's chart that they have developed a safety plan. One of the primary resources for victims is a shelter. Therapists should be familiar with shelters in their area and work with advocates from the shelter to understand their procedures for admitting a victim and to learn how they respond to male victims. You should also have printed materials from the shelter to give to a client who may need to leave an abusive home.

Although in this chapter we list specific suggestions that are included in most safety plans, we recognize that the planning process is unique and that

EXHIBIT 7.2
Sample Detailed Safety Plan

- Make copies of important documents, like birth certificates, marriage certificates, Social Security numbers, medical insurance information, bank account information, and so forth, in case you have to leave the home quickly and need proof of identity or access to money.
- Make an extra set of keys for the home, cars, and so on.
- Keep photocopied documents, extra keys, and some cash and checks hidden in a place that you know and can access quickly if needed (by the door, outside in a hidden spot, in a magnetic key holder attached to the bumper of the car, etc.).
- Have a safe place to go. Make arrangements with a neighbor to be able to go to their house at any time, day or night, if needed. Many arguments occur late at night, or perhaps the offender has taken away keys to prevent the victim from leaving by car. You need to have a place that you or your children can get to quickly.
- Develop a safety plan for your children. Teach them to dial 911 or to go to a neighbor's house where they can be safe. Have a signal between you and your children that you can give if you want them to get out of the house quickly.
- Keep important numbers available: 911, domestic violence shelters, friends or family members, emergency hotlines, for example. If you are unable to call from your home, call as soon as you are safe. We encourage victims to have cell phones.
- Know where all the potential exits and escape routes are in the home, including doors and windows, in case you need to get out of the home quickly. If you feel an attack may be about to begin, make your exit before it starts.
- Do not argue in places where there is only one exit, the room is small and enclosed (for example, the bathroom), or in places like the kitchen, where there are potential weapons. Be sure to stand closest to doorways, where exiting is easier.

---

each client will know what resources are best for her or him. The safety planning process should be considered a structured way to help clients with problem-solving coping skills (Jordan et al., 2004).

TROUBLESHOOTING SAFETY PLANNING

Some clients think safety planning is unnecessary. We want to be strength focused and do not want to discourage them from their hopefulness. However, especially in the group, we have found that most women can understand that even if they feel this is not necessary for themselves, they should recognize that it might become necessary for another group member. We also want to be sure that before we begin conjoint work, we have made every effort to help clients remain safe.

If at the end of a conjoint session, a client feels fearful or reports that tension is escalating at home, we talk about the previously developed plan to help the client consider whether it is still appropriate. For example, if the client anticipated going to the house of a friend and the friend has left the area, a new location may need to be considered. If appropriate, we help them activate their safety plan.

See Exhibit 7.3 for a checklist summarizing key elements of Session 4.

EXHIBIT 7.3
Checklist of Key Elements in Domestic Violence–
Focused Couples Therapy Session 4

1. The session begins with separate-gender meetings.
2. Check-in:
   - Assess risk that may need immediate management.
   - "What have you done well since we last met, and what is not going well yet?"
   - "What parts of the miracle (individual format) or house of a healthy relationship (group format) did you notice in the past week?"
   - Review homework from Session 3, the "Reactions to Anger" worksheet.
3. Teach meditation.
   - Give orientation to meditation practice and rationale for its inclusion in the model.
   - Guide clients in choosing a word or phrase to use for meditation.
   - Practice meditation and respond to client difficulties or questions.
   - Ask clients to practice twice a day for 10 minutes for at least 3 weeks to give meditation a fair try.
4. Safety planning:
   - Explain the rationale for safety planning.
   - Work with clients to plan how to keep themselves and their children safe if their partner becomes violent or threatening.
   - Work with clients to plan how to keep their family safe if they feel in danger of becoming violent or threatening.
5. Session ends with partners meeting together to review briefly the content presented.
   - DO NOT SHARE SPECIFIC SAFETY PLANS IN THE COMBINED GROUP.

8

SESSION 5: ESCALATION AND NEGOTIATED TIME-OUT

The most important thing [about the couples group] was the clarification of the time outs. I felt my husband wouldn't listen to me. I knew they were not being done the way they were taught to be done. But he was very resistant. Somehow by coming here he began to listen. They are saying exactly what I had learned from [the women's group] and what he learned from the men's program. Before this program, he would not even sit there and discuss with me. It was his terms and this was the way it was gonna be. By coming here it was almost like he's listening . . . he listened. . . . He respects me with that now, where before, I wasn't considered.

—Female client

Time out, a common technique included as part of men's batterer treatment, is designed to teach abusive men to monitor their own signs of escalating anger and to interrupt the process that may lead to violence against their partner. When properly employed, time outs allow partners to disengage from the escalating conversation for a period of time and provide a structure for when and how to reintroduce the topic under discussion before the time out was called. It is designed to keep conflict from escalating to violence.

The negotiated time-out session has three goals. First, we teach our clients—male and female—how to recognize signs that they or their partner's anger is beginning to escalate. Second, we help each couple develop their own specific negotiated time-out plan. Finally, we help them develop skills for resolving problems. Having a specific time-out plan in place is a precursor to the conjoint phase of treatment in which we begin to help clients address more challenging issues—issues that may well lead to increased conflict as they are being discussed. Negotiated time-out and learning and practicing Gottman's (1999) skills for resolving solvable problems are strategies the couple can use to manage conflict and have safe and productive discussions of difficult topics.

Before describing how we conduct Session 5, we offer some background on why we developed the time-out lessons the way we did.

CLIENTS' DIFFICULTIES WITH TRADITIONAL
TIME-OUT PROCEDURES

We originally believed that the time-out technique was an effective and useful intervention as traditionally taught. When we originally developed our program, male participants had completed a certified batterer intervention program before coming to our couples program with their partners. We knew they had learned the time-out technique, and we assumed that it was helpful. We were surprised to learn that our female clients tended to lack an understanding of the technique and to view the ways their partners had attempted to use the technique as abusive, especially when men learned the technique in isolation from them, as is common in male batterer programs. Some of our female clients reported that their partners used the technique to control them or to give him an excuse to leave when he wanted to. One woman described this process in the following way:

> [Time outs] really didn't work. When he is really angry and really upset, he still wants to argue and fight. When he's not mad, he pulls a time out just to do something to make me mad and to keep me away.

Women also expressed concern that when their husbands decided to take a time-out, they had no idea when they would return. They were left with all the family responsibilities while the husbands were taking a "break." Some husbands also left and went drinking or engaged in other behaviors that distressed the wives. Some of the husbands told us that they thought they were doing what their anger-management leaders had suggested to keep the intensity of their arguments within safe limits. However, without participating in planning time outs, wives often misunderstood the technique and found the process aversive rather than safety-enhancing.

Women were not the only ones to find time out ineffective. Some male clients reported that time outs did not work before couples counseling. They told us that it was not uncommon for their wives to block their attempts to leave by standing in front of the door or by getting angry at them for abandoning them. One male client told us that whenever he tried to implement time outs, his partner became angry, which made things worse.

She would become aggravated when I left, and when I returned, she was aggravated about whatever the initial problem was, plus she was aggravated that I had left. Eventually, I would just stay away long enough that basically I would just wear her down.

Given the many complaints about time out that couples voiced when we tried to introduce the technique in our initial development of this approach, we realized that we needed to consider other ways it could be implemented. As a result, we developed a process of teaching time out conjointly and helping couples negotiate the parameters of its use, a procedure we came to call *negotiated time-out* (Rosen et al., 2003). This chapter introduces our negotiated time-out procedure and provides insights from our clients on the differences in effectiveness when taught separately in the men's group compared with in a couple's group format. Next, we discuss a procedure that we have introduced more recently, adapted from Gottman's (1999) "Five Skills for Resolving Solvable Problems." This procedure was added to the program to help clients resolve problems when they come back after taking a time out.

SESSION 5 FORMAT AND PROCEDURE

We begin with a separate-gender session. Before presenting the content related to time outs and problem solving, we begin with a 10-minute meditation, ask about any indications of increased risk and of successful interactions in the past week, and use the scaling question to gauge progress. During the separate-gender session, we discuss escalation signals and present an overview of the negotiated time-out process the couples will work on together later in this session. The primary goal of the separate-gender session is to motivate the partners who have had negative experiences with time out to revisit time out in a different way and to explain and get buy-in from clients who have had no experiences with time-outs. As mentioned earlier, many of our clients have had bad experiences with time out and need some assurance that out approach is different. We also encourage clients to view the time out as a safety technique. One client who was resistant to the idea of using the time-out technique reported that when the therapist explained the purpose of time out, he began to see its value:

> Something the therapist said in just the last session was "Maybe all of you don't have a clear idea of what the purpose of the time out is." He said that he recognized that many of us had ideas of what time out was supposed to be, but that we probably didn't have a sole purpose. And then when he said it flat out, he said, "It's safety." And I had to look back and say, well, wait a minute, he's right. I had in my own head that time out is supposed to be something, but when you think about it, he's right. Safety is the number one goal.

Once escalation signals have been discussed and each client has agreed to give the negotiated time-out a try, we spend the rest of the session in a conjoint meeting in which partners work together, with guidance from the therapists, to develop a time-out plan that they believe will work for them. We end the session by teaching clients to use the Gottman (1999) skills for resolving conflicts.

Escalation Signals

The purpose of this discussion is to help clients identify and understand signs they are getting angry or upset so that they can recognize when anger is intensifying. By learning to identify growing intensity early in the cycle, clients are more likely to be able to take steps to manage it effectively. We begin by asking the clients to think about and identify signs that they are getting angry. Through their discussion, and some prompting from the therapists if necessary, the following areas should be covered. In each category we have included some of the common signals our clients report. It is important, however, for each client to recognize the signs that are specific to them and not simply to learn a list of generic signals.

Physical Signals

What are the physical signs that you are getting angry? Some examples might include increased heart rate, increased adrenaline, feeling hot or flushed, red face, tension, muscles tightening, or clenched fists.

Emotional Signals

What are emotional signs of increased anger? Although anger itself is the primary sign, it varies in intensity from mild irritation to rage. Helping clients know the range of angry feelings can be useful. In addition, anger is typically a secondary emotion, and participants can be helped to see other primary emotions that may trigger anger as a secondary reaction, for instance, fear, disappointment, shame, betrayal, disrespect, abandonment, being challenged, jealousy, sadness, and depression.

Thoughts/Self-Talk

Many clients can identify the types of thoughts or self-talk that signal the beginning of an anger or escalation cycle. We use questions such as, "What are the things you tell yourself that may lead you to become angrier? What thoughts seem to signal that you are becoming angry?" Typical client responses include things such as, "Thinking what a jerk my wife is; cursing to myself, name-calling; telling myself I don't have to take this crap."

Behaviors

Clients can also be directed to look for behavioral indications of increased risk or escalation. Typical responses to this question include clenching one's fists, raising one's voice or shouting, pacing, or threatening looks or gestures.

Red-Flag Situations

Up to now, we have asked about internal indicators of increased anger. However, certain situations may signal risk as well. These are situations in which clients know they may more at risk of becoming angry. Helping clients recognize and either control their exposure to such situations or have a safety plan if the situation cannot be avoided is also useful. Some situations that clients have described as red-flag situations are bars or other places or events where alcohol is involved, family gatherings when there is conflict or cutoff, right after work when stress is high, and when discussing money or finances.

Red-Flag Words and Phrases

Certain words or phrases can also serve as triggers for anger or escalation. We ask clients, "What things could someone say to you that are hard to hear and deal with and that might escalate a situation?" Often the response falls into the category of disrespect—for instance, things such as "Shut up!" "What you need to do is . . . " and "You don't know what you're talking about." Another difficult category consists of words or phrases that signal the possibility of emotional abandonment—"I don't love you," "I don't know why I'm in this relationship," or "Only a fool would stay with you." It is important to emphasize to clients that they cannot prevent their partners or others from sometimes saying things that make them angry, and they should not be trying to control what other people do. The goal is to develop a safety plan for managing their own reactions to what they hear so that they keep themselves and those around them safe.

Reactions From Others

Finally, we suggest that our clients become aware of things they observe someone else doing or saying that would let them know that the other person is feeling frightened or threatened. In other words, what reactions of others are signals that the client is getting angry? Typical examples of things our clients observe about their partners are someone backing up from them, someone reacting to them with their own anger, or seeing fear in their face.

Although the discussion of escalation signals can be taught from a didactic perspective, we use a solution-focused approach. This approach relies first on soliciting the experience and knowledge of the clients about what is specific to their own relationships and lives. Thus, instead of presenting a chart of 10 escalation signals, we ask the clients to generate their own list. Questions and suggestions—rather than statements and lectures—can guide the group (or the individual partner) to neglected areas, if there are any. On a more subtle level, the therapists also listen closely to the discussion and highlight or emphasize observations made by clients that illustrate important content areas for that session. In the following transcript, the male therapist, Doug, made a comment about the importance of listening to partners. In response to this comment, one client, "David," became angry. Doug used the solution-focused technique of highlighting exceptions, or building on a comment David made to change the topic from David's partner's flaws to his own increasing self-control:

<table>
<tr><td>Male Client:</td><td>I'm a very good listener. I've listened a lot. And one of the other things that has happened is that as I get more self-control, she's taken it as license to run on and yell and put me down. The night I left it was an hour—an hour and a half just, "You can't do this," and "You're stealing; you might steal from me," and "You're no good." I've never taken anything from her, and I don't have to listen to it, to that. I listen to her when she has a problem, when she has a need, when she needs to tell me something. I've listened to her tons. That's how our relationship got started; I listened to her on the phone, and she thought, "Well, this is wonderful. It's like a free therapist." I listened and listened and listened. I'm not talking about refusing to listen; I'm talking about, I don't have to sit there—I used to try and stop her. You know, I'm not dishonorable. I'm not a crook. [Group laughs.] You know none of these things are true. I've never been arrested. Nothing, nothing.</td></tr>
<tr><td>Male Therapist:</td><td>Let me ask you about one of the other things you said; you said that you feel like you exercise more self-control. You went by that pretty quick. But that's a big thing, and that's really, essentially what this first issue is about, exercising self-control, so I want to ask you a little more about that. It's one thing to say, "I've had more self-control." It's another thing to actually [exercise that self-control]—how have you done that? What sorts of things have helped you exercise more self-control thus far?</td></tr>
<tr><td>Male Client:</td><td>Well I think the main thing is the way we went over signals, physical signals, behavior, like my voice. Like right now [laughs], I can tell I'm getting upset.</td></tr>
</table>

Female Therapist:	But you pulled yourself back. I heard your voice change. So, how did you do that?
Male Client:	Well, I see that I'm getting—I can feel it. We've been talking about it and thinking about it. And then I've gone over things to do. You say, "Well, you didn't mean it." Well, he's probably right; I probably wasn't thinking that way or—[trails off]. So, the reframing, uh, uh, watching for signals, and then deliberate relaxation, and I'm shaking. [Laughs once and then breathes out hard.]
Male Therapist:	I'm going to put up the escalation ladder right now, because it's actually a really good example to use with this. I'm not going to spend much time on this; this goes back to what we were talking about last week, and really this is just a sort of visual way that some people find helpful thinking about conflict escalation.

Here, rather than delivering a lecture or confronting David about the need for him to increase his self-control, the therapist built on the client's strengths and used solution-focused language to lead into a discussion of escalation signals.

The discussion of escalation signals in separate-gender groups sets the stage for the couples working together to design a time-out plan for themselves. The couples come back together as a group (or with their therapists in the single-couple treatment), and the therapists deliver an overview of the negotiated time-out process. Couples are also given handouts to help them develop their plan (Exhibits 8.1 and 8.2), including procedures and a contract. Each couple is then asked to work together to negotiate a time-out plan while the therapists move from couple to couple (in the multicouple group) to provide support and assistance and to monitor the progress of each couple.

Negotiated Time-Out

Although the negotiated time-out procedure that we use to help couples is similar to what is traditionally taught in separate-gender groups, clients in our program learn the technique together, and they have the opportunity to develop their individualized time-out plan, practice it, and receive feedback from the therapist (and other group members in the multicouple group). All clients hear the same information, and they leave the session with a negotiated agreement about when and how time-out is to be used in their relationships. We make the process of developing couple-specific details of the time-out procedure an interactive, negotiation process. We ask couples to practice the technique in session and between sessions, and we use later sessions to

EXHIBIT 8.1
Time-Out Procedures

1. Recognize your feelings. Be aware of your feelings before you get so hot that it's difficult to call a time out.
2. Decide to take a time out. Although ideally the partner who begins to feel the warning signs that anger is beginning to escalate beyond the point where continuation of a discussion would be fruitful, either partner may decide to call a time out.
3. Signal. Either person may signal a time out using a hand gesture, such as a "T" symbol, and in a calm voice, say, "I am going to take a time out."
4. Acknowledge. The other partner acknowledges the person's time out without trying to stop the person or persuade him or her to continue the argument at that time.
5. Disengage. It is important that an angry couple gets out of each other's presence and out of each other's sight during a time out. Go to your predetermined and agreed-on location. Usually, the person calling the time out will go to a specified location while the other partner will stay where he or she is, look after the children, or otherwise steer clear of the partner who called the time out.
6. Cooling off. During the time apart, the partner who called the time out spends time in a designated space doing activities that promote calmness and reduce anger and stress. We encourage you to meditate for at least part of the time you are apart.
7. Return. After the designated period of time, the couple comes back together and decide whether both are calm enough to continue the discussion, if they need to take another time out, drop the issue all together, or want to table the discussion and bring it up again with their therapist at the next meeting or at another mutually agreeable time.

Each step in the time-out procedure is important and should be practiced before it is needed.

EXHIBIT 8.2
Time-Out Contract

1. I pledge to pay attention to my feelings and to call a time out before my anger escalates beyond the point where continuation of a discussion would be fruitful.
2. I will use _____ as a sign that I want to take a time out and will calmly let my partner know that I want to take a time out.
3. I pledge to acknowledge when my partner requests a time out without trying to stop him or her or persuade him or her to continue the argument at that time.
4. The time out will last _____.
5. During the time out, I will _____.
   _____
6. I pledge not to drink alcohol, use drugs, or drive during this time.
7. After the designated period of time, I pledge to return to my partner and jointly decide whether we can renew the discussion, if we need to take another time out, drop the issue all together, or want to table the discussion and bring it up again with our therapist at our next meeting or another mutually agreeable time.

Client Signature_____

revisit and revise the process as needed. We have found that this process increases the likelihood that both partners will follow the plan they developed, and it provides the content around which the couple can build negotiation skills.

We use the following general outline to help couples understand the type of plan we hope they can negotiate.

Step 1: Awareness

Through discussion of escalation signals, we help clients learn to recognize cues that anger is escalating. Partners may have different comfort levels with intense emotion; one may be ready for a time-out before the other has reached his or her warning level. Both partners take ownership for their responses and agree to act in a way that maintains safety. We encourage partners to be vigilant about the earliest signs of escalation when they may be more able to alter the outcome.

Step 2: Staying Within the Safety Zone

Again, we encourage couples to act sooner rather than later to deal with escalation and to use time out when they are in the "safety zone." Rather than waiting until they are out of the safety zone and into the zone of increased risk, we encourage them to use time out when they feel that anger may escalate past the safety zone. Either partner may initiate a time out at this point.

Step 3: Signaling

The initiator signals a time out using a hand gesture, such as a "T" symbol saying in a calm voice, "I am going to take a time out." Partners negotiate what the signal will be and select one that is clear and not threatening. Most of our couples prefer using a hand signal of some kind to using words because increasing anger can make verbal communication difficult or threatening.

Step 4: Acknowledging

The other partner acknowledges the time out. Partners plan ways to resist the urge to continue the argument.

Step 5. Disengaging

Partners go to separate locations. Partners negotiate a specified location, plans for caring for children, and amount of time needed for the time out. It is important that each partner agree on where each of them will go. One man suggested, for instance, that he would like to take his time out at a nearby bar, a suggestion that did not sit well with his wife. We also find that couples differ on the amount of time they believe they will need, but we encourage them to agree on a reasonable time (closer to 1 hour than to 2 days).

Step 6. Cooling Off

The partner who initiates time out spends time doing calming activities. Both partners may need to cool off and may need help finding ways to calm themselves. We recommend that couples practice centering meditations that were taught earlier in the program, but some individuals choose other activities. We encourage them to become involved in activities that distract them so that they do not replay the argument again and again. We encourage them not to use alcohol and not to drive.

Step 7. Returning

Partners check in with each other at the end of the agreed-on period. One of the concerns that many women in our program had with the time-out process was that their partners had requested a time out but never agreed to a "time in" or a time to finish the discussion. We encourage couples to return to the discussion and to take a time in. There are several options at this point. If the partners each feel that they have calmed down sufficiently, they can attempt to continue the discussion. If one or both remain angry and further contact is not advisable, they can take another time out. If the issue is difficult and challenging, they can agree to table it for the time being and raise it with the therapist at their next therapy session. Finally, on occasion couples report that while in time out, they realized that the conflict was really a result of stress or fatigue and that the content they were discussing really had little meaning. Thus, they may decide to drop the issue entirely.

Negotiating Specific Details of the Time Out

After we explain the process, we help couples to negotiate the specific details that work for them. The discussion may begin with both partners describing how they know when they are becoming angry or what signs tell them that their efforts to deal with a conflict are becoming unproductive and unsafe. Therapists need to be active in this discussion, ensuring that the discussion remains productive and not blaming. In addition, therapists need to ensure that decisions about how to use this tool are not made by only one partner. Ensuring that both partners agree to the signal selected, the length of time before checking in, and the activities each will do while separated greatly enhances the likelihood that the procedure is used and is helpful. The therapist is active during this process to make sure that both partners feel heard and can contribute to the decision-making process.

Practice

> I look at it as though it's almost like we're in training. We're getting in shape, we're learning how to do this. At times I get discouraged because my wife wants to jump to the end, and you can't. You have to be ready for it. . . . You need to practice, you need to build strength, you need to work up to it before you go out and run a marathon. It takes a lot of practice and time and you have to be ready for it. (Male client)

Each step in the time-out procedure is important and should be reviewed with the couple and practiced, first during the session and later at home. Practicing the procedure when calm allows couples to think about how predetermined time limits and places of retreat will work in reality. It also underscores the importance of using the tool for safety and more effective problem solving.

Revisit and Revise

Because therapists tell clients from the beginning that they will check in with them about how time out is working, clients know that they will be held accountable for following the agreement they have developed together. Both male and female clients have told us that holding them accountable to follow through on their agreements is helpful. Revisiting the time out in subsequent sessions allows therapists to affirm what is working and to help clients revise parts of the process that are not working.

Rene and Keisha

The following edited transcript illustrates the structure of teaching an individual couple the negotiated time-out procedure:

> *Therapist:* I know you guys have had some struggles with time out in the past, you've talked about that. So today I'm going to teach you a different way to do time out, and I think it's going to be a way that will work better for you, because you're going to both agree beforehand on how time out's going to work. It's also going to be a good tool for helping you get control of the conflicts that are causing you so much trouble, instead of letting those conflicts be in control of you. We're going to just use this as a time to negotiate and figure out a plan that you can go home and try out. Are you willing to give it a try?
>
> *Keisha:* Yeah.
>
> *Rene:* OK.
>
> *Therapist:* OK. Well, one of the first things that we need to talk about is, what are the signals each of you want to use to call a time

out? And we'll begin by looking at how you know when a situation is starting to get to the point where you need some time away to cool down and manage the conflict. Rene, what happens for you?

Rene: Usually I notice . . . I guess my heart rate starts going up a little bit, I start to feel, like I clench my fists, I clench my jaw, and my teeth. So probably more physical signs for me.

Therapist: So you have some really clear physical signs. You start to clench your jaw, your heart rate goes up, and that's when you know, "Something needs to change here or this conflict is going to get out of control."

Rene: Yeah, yeah. Pretty much.

Therapist: Keisha, how about you? What do you see?

Keisha: My mind starts racing, and my speech gets quick, and I get really hot. Then I know it's getting out of control.

Therapist: OK, so you notice your thoughts speeding up, and you start to talk faster, and you get that kind of flushed feeling? OK. Those are great. You guys are really doing a good job of identifying those signals. Now, either of you can call a time out, and you can call it because you feel like you're getting upset, or you can call it because you feel like the situation is getting to the point where you need some time just to get away. But you can't call a time out on each other, OK? I know everybody wants to call a time out on—on their partner, but it's going to be for you. Now that may mean that you see Rene is getting upset and you may say, I need a time out so that I can control myself a little better and think more clearly. And vice versa, Rene, you may see that Keisha's getting upset. So you can—you can call a time out at any time, but it's for your benefit, it's not a blame kind of thing. OK?

Both: OK.

Therapist: So what do you guys want to use as a signal for time out? Lots of people find that it's helpful to use some kind of a physical signal. When you're getting mad, sometimes you're really not able to put that into words so well. A lot of folks use the sports time-out signal [therapist forms a "T" with both hands]. Does that work for you?

Rene: That works for me. I mean that's just the easiest thing to remember. That's like the universal sign for time out.

Therapist:	OK. Keisha, that's OK for you?
Keisha:	Yeah, that works.
Therapist:	So you're going to be aware of those escalation signals. When it hits the point that you've been describing, you're going to use the time-out sign, OK? Then the next step is for the other partner to acknowledge that. So let's say, Keisha, you make the time-out signal. Rene, how can you acknowledge that?
Rene:	Um, I guess just stop, I mean, if we're in the middle of an argument, then just kind of like stop, and that would be my way of acknowledging that we need to separate or whatever.
Therapist:	OK, OK. So you could do it by just breaking off the conversation. Could you do it by saying, "OK, we're in a time out now?"
Rene:	Sure.
Therapist:	Or [makes time-out-signal] doing the sign as well?
Rene:	Alright, yeah.
Therapist:	Sometimes again, a physical sign is a little easier than trying to put into words.
Rene:	So if she does it, then I would do it, too?
Therapist:	Yeah. You would do it, too. Then the next stop in this process is to separate for a little while. Let's think first of all, how long would it make sense for you guys to separate? How long does it take you to cool down, get yourself back under control?
Keisha:	Fifteen or 20 minutes?
Rene:	I'd say, 20 minutes.
Therapist:	Twenty minutes? OK. Keisha, would that be OK with you?
Keisha:	Yeah, we could try that.
Therapist:	Of course. That's a great point. You're going to practice this at home. And we're going to work on it and maybe do some fine-tuning. But let's start with 20 minutes, OK? Where are you going to go?
Rene:	Hmm, maybe to the bar?
Therapist:	Go to the bar . . .

Rene:	It'd be getting away from her.
Therapist:	Well, that's true. Keisha, how would that sit with you?
Keisha:	That doesn't really work for me. [To Rene] You get angrier when you drink.
Therapist:	One of the goals of this is to have a plan put in place before you need it, that both of you know about and both of you feel comfortable with. So today is really a negotiation. I mean, Rene, you might feel more comfortable going to the bar, but if it ends up with leaving Keisha feeling less comfortable, it's not going to serve the purposes that you guys are trying for.
Rene:	OK.
Therapist:	You two live in a house, right?
Keisha:	Yes.
Therapist:	And you've got a second floor maybe, a ground floor and a basement? Are there places in the house that you could get away to?
Rene:	I usually like to step out. Do you think if I took a walk around the block or something?
Therapist:	Check that out with Keisha.
Rene:	What do you think about that, Keisha?
Keisha:	That makes sense, and I could hang out in the basement and cool down.
Therapist:	OK. So Rene you're going to go for a walk, and Keisha you're going to go the basement. [Short pause] What if it's bad weather outside?
Rene:	Hmm. [To Keisha] Well, I guess if you're going to the base-ment, I'll go to the second floor just so that we have some space between us.
Keisha:	A floor between us?
Rene:	Yeah.
Therapist:	OK. So Keisha you're going to go the basement, and Rene you're going to go either for a walk if the weather's nice or . . . do you have a spare room upstairs?
Rene:	Yeah, we have a den upstairs. A computer room.
Therapist:	I know I'm being really picky, but I want you guys to have a clear plan because when you get into this kind of stuff, when

you get into conflicts, it's hard to remember sometimes. I want it to be real clear. And you're going to go downstairs, is there a particular place downstairs, Keisha?

Keisha: We have a couch and a TV down there. So I'll probably just hang out there.

Therapist: OK, let's review. One of you calls a time out and then you're going to separate for 20 minutes. Rene, you're going to either go for a walk, or go upstairs. Keisha, you're going to go to the basement to the couch where the TV is. What are you going to do during the time you're apart in order to calm yourselves down? Sometimes you can keep thinking about what's going on and you can just get madder and madder, right?

Rene: Yes.

Therapist: One of things that we recommend is that you do the meditation that we taught you last session.

Keisha: That makes sense.

Rene: Yeah.

Therapist: Has that been working for you? Is that something that you could try?

Rene: Yeah.

Keisha: Yeah, we can give it a try.

Therapist: So maybe 10 or 15 minutes of meditation. What other things would help you calm down, do you think?

Rene: I have my mp3s on the computer. On the computer in the den. So I could probably listen to some music, that always helps me relax.

Therapist: OK, so music helps you relax. You're not listening to music that gets you more wired up?

Rene: No, I listen to very down tempo stuff.

Therapist: OK. Keisha, what about you?

Keisha: I guess I could turn on the TV or just sit there quietly and relax and maybe keep deep breathing after my meditation.

Therapist: Are there any other things that might help you if you're really upset? I mean, those are great things, don't get me wrong.

Keisha: For me, maybe making some tea and sitting with that warm tea . . .

Therapist:	Alright. So when the 20 minutes is over, then it's time for what we call "time in." One of the complaints that people have about time out is you call a time out and you never come back then to talk about the issue until it comes up the next time you've got a conflict. So then we do time in, and at that point I want you guys to get back together, and you can make three choices at that point. One is, we've calmed down enough, let's try and talk about this. The second choice . . . well, actually there are four choices . . . the second choice is sometimes couples get back together and they say, "Why we were we getting so upset about that? It's not that big a deal." Have you guys had that experience?
Keisha:	Yeah.
Rene:	A lot.
Therapist:	So the second choice is you can say, we don't need to go back to this, this was silly. Both of you have to agree about that, though. Rene, if you think it's silly, and Keisha thinks it's serious, then you have to go back to the issue and see if you can settle it. Got it?
Keisha:	Yeah.
Therapist:	The third thing you can do is say, I think we need to talk about this but I'm still pretty upset, let's take another time out, let's take another 20 minutes. And the fourth choice . . . sometimes you guys may run into a problem that gets you going so much, you may want to table it, and bring it into the next therapy session. Sometimes families have these kinds of huge issues or couples have these huge issues that are really hard to, you know, hard to deal with, and so we encourage you to use the therapy sessions that way too. Does that all make sense to you guys?
Both:	Yeah.
Therapist:	OK, then run through the steps for me, tell me what you're going to do.
Keisha:	Well, we're going to have a fight [everyone laughs], and we're going to feel the things that tell us we're escalating.
Rene:	And once we notice those signs, we'll take a time out by using the time-out signal.
Keisha:	And I'll time out you back. [makes a T with her hands]
Rene:	The other person will acknowledge and then we'll separate. I'll go either outside and take a walk for 20 minutes or I'll

go upstairs into the computer room and she'll go into the basement.

Keisha: And then we come back together and decide if we can talk about it or if it's something we just don't need to talk about, that it's not a big issue after all.

Rene: If we need more time then we'll take another time out.

Therapist: OK, if you need more time.

Keisha: Or bring it to therapy.

Therapist: Great job. Now this is going to seem silly. Or it seems silly to some people, but I want you to each call a time out this coming week when you're not mad.

Rene: [Quizzically] OK?

Therapist: As kind of practice, you know. Because again, once you get into those conflicts, your emotions take over, the intensity gets high. I want you to practice a little bit. It's just like practicing, you know, for a sporting event. The first time you play sports isn't in the big stadium where everybody's cheering. You start with practice so you can really focus on learning the steps. So, are you willing to give that a try?

Rene: Sure.

Therapist: OK. Go through all the steps. OK? And that will help us figure out if there are things that we need to fine-tune or work on next time, so.

Both: OK.

Therapist: I'm impressed. You're really thoughtful. You've got some good clues about what the escalation signals are. You've got a good plan. And this can really help you gain control of those conflicts. Right now those conflicts are controlling your relationship.

Both: Yeah.

Clients' Experience of Negotiated Time-Out

As mentioned earlier, throughout our development of the treatment program described in this book, we conducted research interviews with clients and therapists. Although our research protocol did not have specific questions about time out, many clients mentioned this procedure unprompted. Couples told us that they found this time out be helpful because it was adapted to fit their needs. In fact, for some couples, negotiating an agreement about how and when to use time out was one of the highlights of their treatment. In the quotes that follow, a male client describes how revisiting the time-out procedure and learning by watching other couples who did, or did not, use it was helpful for him.

> Like I said, the suggestion of the time-out procedures, that was something. When I first talked to [wife] about time out, she's like, you won't use it, so it won't work. And I would persist a little further, and that stuff was from anger management, as soon as we got to family counseling, it was about the second or third session that [wife] recognized that [another couple in group] were using the time-out procedure, but then on the other hand, she saw how [a different couple in the group] weren't using the time-out procedure. They hadn't even sat down and talked about it. So, she saw how one couple used it and it was working, the other couple, it wasn't working. That's what I meant when I said that having the couples there interact, she can see the negative and the positive. That to me was extremely helpful. I remember looking at her face when she saw how [the first couple] were getting along using their time-out procedure. Now, all of a sudden she says to me that weekend that followed that session, "time out." And I was like, "huh?" "What?" [laughs]. "OK!" I saw my wife open up, like I said, you just turn on a green light from a stop light. Then that following weekend, she called a time out, and she has never ever done that. Never. Made me feel really good. To me, that's what the family counseling did.

One aim of helping couples negotiate a useful time-out plan is maintaining safety. Another aim is to help partners resolve their conflicts more effectively, because little useful communication takes place when tempers flare. For example, one male client spontaneously told us during one of his interviews that when he and his wife began using time out effectively, they began to resolve their conflicts more readily:

> When we started, [use of time out] was zero! I would follow her around the house, yelling and screaming. She'd be yelling and screaming, the kids would be crying. Now we're able to come back [after a time out], level-headed and calm, and I'd say 90% of the time we'll resolve [the issue].

Clients also saw the benefit of working together to develop the time-out plan. One male client told us:

> In the anger management, I learned time out. It would have been helpful if my wife had been to anger management and learned time out also. What was nice was [in the couples program] we got together and we discussed time out in two of the sessions, we got it really clear, what we were going to do.

Clients' confidence in the process grows as they are able to use it successfully or as they hear how other couples in the group have used it to manage conflict. Another male client reported this:

> We actually had a pretty smooth week. But, there were one or two times when we just kind of went in the other room kind of thing. And, at one point my wife wanted to talk about it, I said no, and she respected that. That felt really good. So, that was very effective to work on the larger problems, and that made a really good trend.

Teaching this tool also provides an opportunity to help couples negotiate. A crucial aspect of this process is an active, directive therapist who alternates between partners to allow both to express their preferences and to help them hear each other. With guidance, couples can develop an agreement that reflects what they both want and can experience a process that may be new to them—that is, respectful negotiation. This sets the stage for tackling more difficult couple issues in the conjoint phase of treatment.

STARTING A DIFFICULT CONVERSATION

Once a couple learns how to use the time out to deescalate conflict, it is important to work with them on how to start a difficult conversation. If the previous conversation about the topic led to escalation and the need to take a time out, it is likely that the topic is a difficult one for the couple to discuss. Therefore, we teach our clients to use concepts from Gottman's (1999) "Five Skills for Resolving Solvable Problems," found in his book *The Marriage Clinic: A Scientifically Based Marital Therapy*, to help them enhance their communication skills and be able to discuss difficult issues. For more detailed information on this procedure, we encourage you to read Gottman's book. We use three of the five steps recommended by Gottman to teach clients how to approach difficult conversations.

Softened Start-Up

We begin by introducing the concepts of harsh and gentle start-ups. Some rules for softened start include the following: "In the initial start-up sentence, complain but do not blame; start with something positive; describe what is happening, don't evaluate or judge; be polite, express appreciation, restate your feelings in terms of more vulnerable emotions, and use 'I' statements" (Gottman, 1999, p. 226). We explain the difference between "I" and "you" statements. Couples are instructed to use "I" statements to explain to one another how they feel about a certain issue. They are discouraged from using "you" statements, which often cast blame on the partner. To help the couple develop softened start-up skills, we provide the couple with examples of harsh start-ups. The following is an example from Gottman's (1999) book:

> Topic: Your partner's car has a new dent in it. You are concerned that your partner is not being a careful driver and worried about your partner's safety.
>
> Harsh start-up: I saw that new dent. When are you going to stop being so reckless?
>
> Softened alternative: I saw that new dent. What happened? I am really getting worried about your driving, and I want you to be safe. Can we talk about this? (p. 224)

After we have given them examples, we provide examples of harsh start-ups and have each individual practice a softened start-up and coach them as they learn this skill. In the group, other group members help in the coaching process.

Repair and Deescalation

Once clients are able to approach a conversation using the softened start-up, we move to Step 2 of Gottman's (1999) model. When clients come back after a time out, it is likely that there is some negativity surrounding the issue that led them to choose to use a time out. It is important to help clients learn to repair the negativity. This is done by again reiterating the importance of "I" versus "you" statements. Clients are encouraged to share how they feel and to take responsibility for their actions. If the conflict escalated before time out, it may be necessary for one or both partners to apologize for their previous behavior. It is important to work with the couple on approaching the issue by repairing the negativity and beginning to discuss the issue more positively.

We practice this with clients by having them discuss a previous conflict. We ask them to practice with a minor conflict, not a highly volatile ongoing one. They are encouraged to first repair the negativity and use "I" statements to softly begin the conversation. The recipient of the repair attempt is encouraged to provide positive feedback to the partner after the attempt to repair the negativity. The purpose of this is so that the partner repairing the negativity knows that this effort is accepted and appreciated. Again, we observe the interaction and point out times when the conversation turns to negative, or blaming, language.

Accepting Influence

The next step of our adaptation of Gottman's (1999) model is "Accepting Influence." In this step, couples learn how to "find those parts of their partner's position that they can understand and with which they can agree" (p. 233). For conflicts that are not "gridlocked" (p. 233), partners learn that sharing or relinquishing power can improve their marriage.

In this exercise, couples work together to develop a common way of thinking about an issue and begin coming up with compromises. They seek to find common feelings, goals, and methods for accomplishing these goals. Clients learn how to discuss their position on an issue and make a decision that both individuals agree with. Again, we emphasize using positive language to explain one's position and to avoid casting blame or negativity on the other person. Clients learn to listen carefully to the other's position and to identify where compromise is possible.

Learning to accept influence is an important step of communication for couples who often leave conflicts unresolved. These skills allow couples to discuss an issue calmly and reach decisions that are normally difficult for them to make. By successfully completing this step, couples are empowered by their ability to discuss issues and reach mutual decisions.

Although we encourage clients to use Gottman's (1999) Five Skills for Resolving Solvable Problems regularly, our experience is that many have gotten into patterns of escalating conflict. A key aspect of our model is helping clients negotiate a time out that allows them to deescalate. While they are calming down, we encourage them to meditate or use other calming strategies. Before they reconnect, they are encouraged to think about a way to reconnect and complete a discussion, if possible. They are encouraged to think of using a softened start-up, begin the connecting with a repair attempt, and to think of a way they might be able to accept influence or support some aspect of their partner's position. Although this process is taught in this session, we revisit both the negotiated time-out and the skills for resolving conflict as needed throughout the program. Exhibit 8.3 is a checklist summarizing key elements of Session 5.

EXHIBIT 8.3
Checklist of Key Elements in Domestic Violence–Focused Couples Therapy Session 5

1. The session begins with separate-gender meetings.
2. Lead meditation for 10 minutes.
   - Briefly discuss meditation experiences over the past week.
3. Check-in:
   - Assess risk that may need immediate management.
   - "What have you done well since we last met, and what is not going well yet?"
   - "What parts of the miracle (individual format) or house of a healthy relationship (group format) did you notice in the past week?"
4. Prepare for conjoint negotiated time-out planning.
   - Acknowledge prior negative experiences with time out.
   - Present material on escalation signals and guide clients to identify their escalation signals.
5. Conjoint session: negotiated time-out planning:
   - Present rationale for negotiated time-out.
   - Guide couples in developing a time-out plan.
   - Use handouts if desired to provide structure.
   - Discuss strategies for returning to a difficult conversation after time out.
6. Homework:
   - Each partner practices calling a time out when neither is angry.

9

SESSION 6: ALCOHOL AND DRUG USE

Substance abuse and intimate partner violence (IPV) co-occur with significant frequency. Foran and O'Leary (2008), on the basis of a meta-analytic review, reported an association between alcohol use and both male-to-female IPV and female-to-male IPV. Although much of the research has focused on alcohol, a growing body of research suggests that the use of illicit substances is also associated with IPV (Chermack & Blow, 2002; Chermack, Fuller, & Blow, 2000; Kantor & Straus, 1989; Moore & Stuart, 2004).

The research literature is certainly in line with our clinical experience. In the early days of developing our model, we decided that we would not work with couples in which one or both partners had a substance abuse problem. We were afraid that substance abuse would interfere with successful treatment of IPV. We used standard screening instruments—the Michigan Alcohol Screening Test and the Drug Abuse Screening Test—with all of our incoming clients to assess their levels of substance abuse. Based only on the scores on these instruments, we quickly found that we were excluding almost everyone who was seeking treatment in our program. However, when we conducted clinical assessments with the same clients, we found that many of them were in successful recovery or had not had significant substance abuse problems for some time. In addition, we found that a number of clients who entered domestic violence–focused couples therapy (DVFCT) and had substance abuse issues that they had not disclosed to us were able to work successfully in the program. The screening tests, of course, generally ask about lifetime occurrences of substance abuse problems, and we were more interested in our clients' current patterns of use. Thus, we amended our exclusion criteria to exclude only couples in which either partner has an active, untreated substance abuse problem. Given the realities of the co-occurrence of substance use and abuse and IPV, to exclude all couples with problems with substances would have resulted in a model applicable to only a small number of couples. If we are working with IPV issues, we are working with substance abuse problems as well. The question for us became how to do so safely and with appropriate attention to the substance abuse issues our clients brought with them.

As we described in Chapter 2 on assessment, our screening criteria result in a population of clients who are appropriate for Alcohol Use Disorders Identification Test (Babor, Higgins-Biddle, Saunders, & Monteiro, 2001) Zone 1 (Alcohol Education) or Zone 2 (Simple Advice) interventions and within the range of "monitoring and reevaluation" on the Drug Abuse Screening Test—10th edition (Skinner, 1982). Those with more severe levels of substance abuse will either already be involved in primary substance abuse treatment or will be excluded from DVFCT. Thus, we adopted a motivational interviewing (Miller & Rollnick, 2002) style approach to our substance abuse module. The module is designed to help clients evaluate their own substance use and decide what changes, if any, they would like to make. Because of the close association between substance abuse and IPV, we recommend that participants in the program eliminate all use of alcohol, illicit drugs, or prescription drugs not being used as prescribed during the course of treatment. This remains a recommendation. We do not conduct urinalyses or otherwise routinely monitor our participants' substance use. As noted earlier, relapses may or may not result in discontinuation of DVFCT, depending on the nature and extent of the relapse, its association with any increased risk of violence (e.g., intense couple conflict about the relapse, recurrence of violence or extensive verbal abuse, other out-of-control behavior), and whether the client continues in primary substance abuse treatment.

We have incorporated several motivational interviewing principles in our substance abuse module. First, we emphasize client autonomy. We make clear that the clients are in charge of which changes, if any, they decide to make. We ask them to do their own self-assessment and change plan privately, and we do not ask what they decide or monitor their progress. Second, we try to express empathy for clients' experience by making room to talk about both the pros and cons of using substances. If we leave the benefits of substance use out of the conversation, we have not truly understood our clients and the depth of their struggle to decide what to do about substance use. It is rare that treatment professionals talk about the benefits of substance use. When clients truly feel you are interested in their experience and will not be punitive in your response, they can describe a number of benefits. Substance use can dampen anxiety, increase social comfort, and help control trauma symptoms. Some substances just create an overall good feeling when clients use them. In some relationships, substance use can be the occasion for talking about issues that otherwise are too difficult or are habitually avoided. Therapists must be careful not to undermine this discussion by immediately pointing out the downsides of substance use or reminding clients that many of the benefits are temporary. The conversation does not stop with the benefits. We ask clients to generate a list of the disadvantages or harmful aspects of substance use as well. Much like asking about suicide will not lead clients to make suicide attempts if they are not already considering such actions, leaving room for talking about the benefits of substance use will not encourage more substance use or lead clients to misuse substances if they are not already doing so.

Finally, we try to not engender resistance if we can help it and to "roll with resistance" when it does arise. Thus, we remind clients that they make their own choices, we provide information in a clear and objective manner, and we try our best not to be drawn into arguments.

SESSION 6 FORMAT AND PROCEDURE

Session 6 is conducted with partners separated. We begin with the regular check-in process described in Chapter 6. Before moving on to the content of the session, we also lead the clients in a 10-minute meditation.

Talking about drug and alcohol use is difficult for most people because it is perceived as both private and potentially shameful. In families, or between friends, conversations about substance use often occur when someone perceives a problem. These conversations quickly develop a blaming, defending, or otherwise negative tone. This can carry over into therapy where clients expect to be judged and confronted when therapists ask about their use of alcohol and drugs. This has often resulted in an experience that therapists call resistance or denial and clients often call being harassed and misunderstood. All of us tend to reject input that appears to threaten our freedom, a concept called *psychological reactance* (Brehm & Brehm, 1981). Thus, clients who are ordered to come to therapy have a harder time participating productively compared with those who choose to come. Medical patients tend to comply less fully with treatment when they feel they do not have control over their health care decisions. Warning labels on movies and television shows actually increase the desire for people to view violent programs—the "forbidden fruit" phenomenon. Accordingly, we want both to talk about alcohol and drug use and its consequences for our clients and to be absolutely clear that they make the final decision about what, if anything, they do about it.

This module includes a number of exercises—too many to include in a single session. Therapists can choose which exercises to use on the basis of their assessment of the client's needs and the openness of the relationship. When clients are comfortable with the therapist and the therapeutic process and fairly nondefensive, therapists can use the more interactive exercises. These are exercises that involve discussion of personal use and opinions with the therapist or in the group. Clients who are less open might do better with some of the individually completed exercises. These exercises involve things such as paper-and-pencil worksheets that do not require a self-disclosure on the part of the clients. We would recommend that the Awareness Window and Planning for the Future (Exhibit 9.1) exercises be done if at all possible.

Introducing the Topic of Substance Use and Domestic Violence

We start by telling clients that today's topic is sometimes a difficult one—one that many people find hard to talk about. We ask what their experience with having conversations about alcohol and drug use has been. Several themes may emerge. Some conversations about substance use have bragging as their focus: "I can drink more than you," or "You wouldn't believe how stoned I was last Saturday." Other conversations focus on concealing how much one is using—evading the issue. Finally, some conversations in the past will have been accusatory, with other people telling the client that they are misusing drugs or alcohol in a variety of ways. We try to draw out these (and other) themes without letting the client lapse into elaborate storytelling. When the themes are out on the table, we tell them that the purpose of this session is not bragging, evading, or blaming. Rather, we have a different goal in mind. We have a clear recommendation that people in high-conflict relationships abstain from alcohol and drugs. However, that is our idea, and they are the only ones who can choose whether that fits for them. Today's session is designed to help them think about the pros and cons of their own substance use and decide what, if anything, they want to do about it. We start by giving our rationale for including a session on substance abuse in DVFCT. We present the following information to the clients in both a short therapist-led presentation and a handout.

- Alcohol use is often associated with domestic violence. Alcohol is present in more than 50% of all incidents of domestic violence.

EXHIBIT 9.1
Planning for the Future Worksheet

After the discussion of drug and alcohol use in group tonight and thinking about the pros and cons of your own use of alcohol or drugs, what do you see as the balance of costs and benefits of using alcohol and drugs in your life?

__ Costs far outweigh the benefits.
__ Cost somewhat outweigh the benefits.
__ Benefits and costs about the same.
__ Benefits somewhat outweigh the costs.
__ Benefits far outweigh the costs.

If you were to make one change in your drinking or drug use that would improve your situation, what would it be? Describe the change as specifically as you can: "cut down," "stop altogether," and so on.

If you made this change, what benefits, if any, do you think you would see in your relationship in 6 months?

What would be the downside of making this change?

Right now, on a scale from 1 to 10 how **important** is making this change to you?

Write the number here _____

Where:

1 = *Not at all important*

10 = *Extremely important*

Right now on a scale from 1 to 10, how much **desire** do you have to make this change?

Write the number here ___

Where:

1 = *I really have no desire to make this change.*

10 = *Making this change is my number 1 priority.*

Right now, on a scale from 1 to 10, how **confident** are you that you could make *and* maintain this change if you decided to make it?

Write the number here ___

Where:

1 = *Not at all confident*

10 = *Completely confident*

What might get in the way of you making and maintaining this change if you decided to do so?

You can use your answers on this worksheet to consider whether you want to make a change in your use of drugs and alcohol. Remember, however, that making a change, no matter what it is, is up to you.

- Individuals appear to be more at risk of injury by domestic violence (and other causes, for that matter) if they have been using. It is a risk factor for injury.
- Research on alcohol abuse and domestic violence makes it clear that people with drinking problems are at high risk of being abusive toward their partners. However, it is also clear that many people who have drinking problems do not abuse their partners and that some people who do not have drinking problems do abuse their partners.
- Given this, why do we recommend abstinence? Because alcohol and drug use is known to impair thinking and judgment, produce changes in mood and behavior, reduce inhibition, and increase aggression. We're taking the "safe rather than sorry" route.

Basic Information About Drug and Alcohol Use and Abuse

After giving our rationale for talking about substance use and abuse, we move on to some basic issues. We want to define what we mean by *substance abuse* so that we have a common basis for discussion. This information may be especially useful to present to individuals in whom there is a fair amount of denial about drug and alcohol use, but we try to do so carefully because it can easily lead to labeling, arguing, and other resistance-arousing interactions. We cover what constitutes a "standard drink" and what constitutes the abuse of alcohol and other drugs.

We start with a standard drink chart that describes clearly what we mean when we say "a drink" because interpretations of what constitutes a drink of alcohol can vary widely. Such charts are freely available from the National Institutes on Alcohol Abuse and Alcoholism (NIAAA) and other such agencies. We then present the NIAAA standards for risky drinking. This has two aspects. *High volume risky drinking* occurs when men drink 14 or more standard drinks in a week and when women drink seven or more standard drinks in a week. *High quantity risky drinking* occurs when men have four or more standard drinks in a day and when women have three or more in a day. It is important to emphasize that there are situations in which having even less alcohol can represent risky drinking—for example, when driving, while pregnant, and in situations in which coordination and good judgment are required for safety. We ask the clients either to discuss (if the group or individual has not been defensive about the topic) or silently consider (if the group or individual has been defensive) where they each fall individually on these standards. Those who exceed both the single day and weekly limits are at the highest risk, those who exceed either the weekly or daily limits are at increased risk, and those who abstain from alcohol or do not exceed the limits above are at low risk.

Next we discuss the CAGE screening questions (Mayfield, McLeod, & Hall, 1974) as another way to help clients see whether they appear to have a substance abuse problem. These questions are as follows:

C—Have you ever thought you should CUT DOWN on your drinking or drug use?

A—Have you ever felt ANNOYED by others' criticism of your drinking or drug use?

G—Have you ever felt GUILTY about your drinking or drug use?

E—Do you have a morning EYE OPENER? (Especially with alcohol)

In group, we use the CAGE by having each member write down his or her answers privately as the therapist reads the questions. We do not have the clients report their answers out loud. Having to make one's answers public can lead to the evading or arguing posture described earlier. We remind the clients that this information is for their use only. After the clients have responded to the questions, we give them the following information: "Two or more positive answers are associated with a diagnosis of dependence for alcohol in 90% of cases and likely indicative of a similar level of difficulty with other drugs. One positive answer may indicate a problem."

Because there are no guidelines for the "safe" use of illicit drugs, we use another strategy to help clients think about the role of all psychoactive substances in their lives. This exercise asks clients to look at the amount of energy that goes into their use of drugs and alcohol and how that may impinge on other important areas in their lives. We introduce this exercise by saying something such as, "Another way to think about alcohol and drug use is based on its effects across many areas of your life, not only on the quantity you use."

We then use the Circle Diagram to illustrate (Figure 9.1). The therapist can either draw this on the board or give a copy to the client.

We introduce the Circle Diagram by saying something such as:

As substance use becomes more problematic, it begins to be more and more of a focus in one's life, gradually taking precedence over other things. People begin to prefer the substance to friends, family, work, recreation, spiritual activities, and so on. At its worst, people will sacrifice all other aspects of their lives for the relationship with the drug. The top circle shows a life that has good balance with appropriate amounts of energy going to a variety of important parts of a person's life. The bottom circle shows how life can get out of balance when too much energy is going to only one thing—in this case, drugs or alcohol—and thereby taking away energy from other important things, such as work or family. I want each of you to think about your own life and the place that drugs and alcohol play in it. Which circle is more like your life?

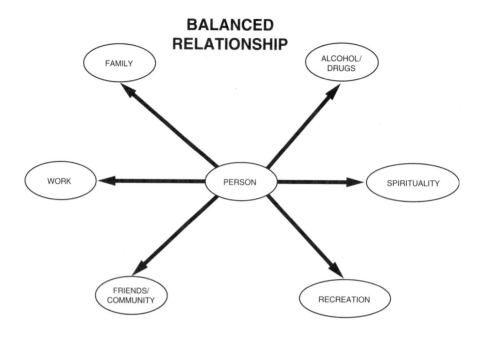

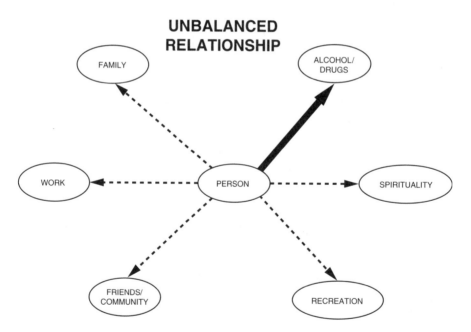

Figure 9.1. Balanced and unbalanced relationship diagrams.

If it appears that discussion would not raise too much defensiveness, we then ask clients to discuss this, drawing parallels to their own lives if they want or to people they know or have heard about—the movie star who lets his career go down the tubes because of drug use, the family member who has a difficult marriage because he or she prefers to use, and so on.

The final part of the session involves helping clients make a more personal assessment of the part that drugs and alcohol play in their lives and also make a commitment to action, if they so choose. We introduce this section with a statement something such as:

> The rest of the session will focus on how drugs and alcohol fit into your own life. Remember, this is a chance for you to take a clear look at the role drugs and alcohol play for you. Only you can decide what you do with the information you discover.

Personal Assessment and Commitment

We choose from one of the following exercises, depending on your assessment of what will fit best for the client or the group. The Awareness Window depends more on therapist–client interaction and would be preferable, whereas using the written inventories may be more helpful with a client or group that is more reticent to talk or more defensive. However, the consequences inventories do not allow for discussion of the positive side of alcohol and drug use, so the therapists will need to promote some discussion of that as well.

Substance Abuse and My Life

The premise of this exercise is to have clients reflect on the following question: What are the consequences of alcohol and drug use in my life?

We ask clients to fill out privately the Short Inventory of Problem (SIP), an inventory of the consequences of alcohol or drug use. The SIP is available at no cost from the Center on Alcoholism, Substance Abuse and Addictions at the University of New Mexico (http://casaa.unm.edu). We remind clients that even though the SIP references drinking, we want them to consider the use of all drugs as they answer. When clients or groups are finished, we ask them to share what they wish. We try to stimulate discussion with questions such as: "Looking it over, did anything surprise you?" "How would you summarize the consequences of alcohol and drug use in your life?" and "What are some of the positive things about drug and alcohol use that aren't in the questions?"

Awareness Window Exercise: The Good and Not-So-Good Things About Drug and Alcohol Use

The Awareness Window exercise is designed to help clients explore the positive and negative consequences of drug and alcohol use with a particular focus on nonviolence and family relationships. It will also help clients examine their own conflicting thoughts and feelings about their substance use. We have adapted this exercise from Ingersoll, Wagner, and Gharib (2002).

We begin by drawing the Awareness Window diagram on a flip chart or blackboard. It is best to do the exercise with the therapist writing the client's responses on a flip chart, especially in the group format, because this keeps all members involved in the process. The diagram is a simple 2-by-2 box. The columns are labeled "Good Things" and "Not So Good Things," and the rows are labeled "Short Term" and "Long Term." The client can also be given a copy of the Awareness Window drawn on a piece of paper to complete privately if the therapist thinks this would be more effective.

We introduce the exercise by saying something like the following:

> We're going to use the Awareness Window to look at both the positive and negative aspects of drug and alcohol use. You might be surprised to hear us say we will talk about the positive aspects of substance use but the truth is that no one would use drugs or alcohol if there were no good things about using them, and we want you to be realistic about your own choices. Like many things, drugs and alcohol have benefits and side effects.

We begin by filling out the Awareness Window with Awareness of Good Things. We ask the clients to contribute some of the good short-term aspects of drug and alcohol use and then move on to the long-term aspects. It is especially important for the therapists to try to head off the "bragging" aspects of talking about substance abuse when talking about the good things. However, we have found that talking about the positive aspects of substance use in a treatment setting is such a novel experience that it is often accompanied by a fair amount of humor. As long as it remains appropriate, it can set the stage for a more open discussion of the disadvantages of substance use.

When the client or group has generated a list of good things, we move on to not-so-good things. We repeat the process with the client generating items for the chart. Here it is important to avoid the "blaming" aspect of discussing substance use. Be careful to avoid labeling responses (e.g., "That sounds like a real problem"). When the chart is done, ask some variant of the following question if it has not already come up.

> Now that you are seeing both the good things and the not-so-good things about drug and alcohol use, how are you reacting to this topic? What has this session been like for you? How are you feeling in general about exploring these issues?

This sets the stage for the "Planning for the Future" exercise.

Planning for the Future Exercise

This exercise is the last activity in the session, and it is conducted by each client privately. It involves a self-assessment and planning for the future exercise. We introduce this exercise by saying something such as:

> It is entirely up to you what you do about your use of alcohol or other drugs in your life. Other people may offer you advice (we, for instance, advise couples in whom there has been abuse to abstain from any drug or alcohol use), but only you can balance the pros and cons of using drugs or alcohol in your life. We will ask you to do the following exercise privately, and then you may share as much or as little of it as you wish.

We then ask the clients to fill out the Planning for the Future Worksheet privately (Exhibit 9.1).

When clients are done, ask them to share as much or as little as they wish. Then have them seal the worksheet in an envelope and sign their name across the back. Tell them that you will give the unopened envelope back to them at the end of therapy so that they can use it as a way to review and remind themselves of what they decided during this session.

TROUBLESHOOTING SESSION 6

Therapists use their judgment as to whether to conduct Session 6. If the therapist is working with a single couple and neither one has a problem with drugs or alcohol, this session is omitted, and the conjoint session of the program includes 13 sessions. Sometimes we have decided that we wanted more time to review some of the aspects of the first 5 weeks and have continued this work before beginning the conjoint phase in Session 7 with clients having no problems with drugs or alcohol.

More judgment is needed when determining how to handle Session 6 when some couples have problems and others do not. If only one or a few couples have a problem, we have sometimes asked them to come to an extra session where this material is addressed. We have also presented this session to the entire group and talked about how common this problem is in our society and asked them to consider how this material might help them understand family members, friends, or colleagues with these types of problems. Most group members realize that everything addressed in group may not pertain to them but that as group members they can be helpful to others.

See Exhibit 9.2 for a checklist summarizing key elements of Session 6.

EXHIBIT 9.2
Checklist of Key Elements in Domestic
Violence–Focused Couples Therapy Session 6

1. Session begins with separate-gender meetings.
2. Check-in:
   - Assess risk that may need immediate management.
   - "What have you done well since we last met, and what is not going well yet?"
   - "What parts of the miracle (individual format) or House of a Healthy Relationship (group format) did you notice in the past week?"
   - Review homework from Session 5—negotiated time-out practice.
3. "Talk about talking about" substance abuse.
   - Describe typical ways of talking about substance abuse.
   - Set the stage for a less defensive experience.
4. Provide information about relationship of substance abuse and intimate partner violence.
5. Choose which of the exercises in the chapter to use.
   - Assess the needs and openness of the clients.
6. Provide basic information on substance abuse and acceptable levels of use.
7. Guide clients in personal assessment of their own substance use.
   - For abstinent clients, invite them to use another bothersome behavior as the content for this exercise.
8. Guide clients in making a personal plan for future change.
9. Collect written plans in sealed envelopes to be returned at the end of the program.

10

SESSIONS 7 THROUGH 18:
PHASE 2—CONJOINT TREATMENT

Anger management made a big difference in my life, but what's nice about the family counseling is having the women there. I mean, let's face it, it takes two to tango. And the women have just as much right and just as much say so in an argument as the men do. There's always two sides to every story. I think it's great they come together. Both sides need to talk. They need to air the things that are bothering them.

—Male client

Phase 2 of domestic violence–focused couples therapy (DVFCT) involves a shift in focus on two fronts. First, we move from a primary focus on working separately with male and female partners to working conjointly. As we describe later, safety remains a primary focus throughout DVFCT; therefore, we always have the option to meet separately if we believe it is necessary to manage risk or otherwise maintain safety. However, during Phase 2, we begin to help couples address some of the issues that they wish to change in their relationship. Although this may seem like a shift away from our focus on violence, it usually is not. Instead, we begin to help couples work on the situations and issues that create the conflict from which violence can erupt. We encourage couples to go slowly in this process. For instance, we helped one couple address some smaller and more easily resolved issues early in the conjoint phase so that they could have the experience of successfully managing differences before they took on what they described as the "nuclear issue"—a very charged conflict between the husband and the wife's extended family. Having a foundation of success with less difficult issues allowed this couple eventually to be success- ful at managing the issue that had caused them the most conflict and that had led to violence. Not only does this work help couples deal with the specific conflicts they are experiencing in the present, it also allows them to learn strategies that will help them in the future as they encounter other difficult life circumstances.

The second shift in focus is from a primarily therapist-directed process to a client-directed process. Whereas the content for the first 6 weeks is set largely by the therapists using a primarily psychoeducational approach, in Phase 2, the clients' goals and issues become the focus. The therapists clearly remain active in Phase 2, but they may not be as directive as they were in Phase 1. As we describe later, the therapists may step back into a more directive role if there are indications of increased risk, if couples report further abusive interactions, if couples are not effectively using skills from Phase 1, or if other circumstances suggest more direct intervention by the therapists.

We begin this chapter with a review of the mechanisms in place to reduce risk and help maintain safety. We then describe the solution-focused model in more detail and the solution-focused principles that guide our work. Finally, we describe the later stages of the conjoint phase in which changes are solidified and plans for the future are made.

FOUNDATIONS OF SAFETY DURING CONJOINT TREATMENT

Phase 1 of DVFCT represents our effort to put in place what we think of as foundations of safety that will allow us to move to working with the couple together with as much assurance of safety as we can provide. No treatment of any kind can guarantee the safety of any participant, and clients need to know this at the beginning. We have certainly worked with couples in which violence has recurred over the course of DVFCT treatment. However, we believe that skilled therapists, working within a structure that is specifically designed to assess and manage risk, can reduce the likelihood of couples' aggression recurring. To that end, we believe the following things are essential for the conjoint work to proceed.

1. We do not begin the conjoint phase of treatment until both partners in separate-gender sessions have signed a no-violence contract and have independently developed and agreed to implement a safety plan if the threat of violence should recur. We recognize that the no-violence contract is mostly symbolic. We assume that our clients want to end the violence. If it were as simple as signing a contract, they would have already stopped the violence. However, the no-violence contract makes ending violence a focus of treatment. No-violence contracts are signed by both partners at the initiation of Phase 1, and safety plans are developed in Week 3, as we described earlier.

EXHIBIT 10.1
Postsession Safety Questionnaire

Date: _____ Client # _____ Session # _____ Client Gender: Male   Female

Please circle the most appropriate response to each of the questions below.

1. How certain are you that YOUR PARTNER will <u>not</u> be physically violent toward you between now and the next time we meet?

1	2	3	4
Very certain	Fairly certain	Somewhat uncertain	Very uncertain

2. How certain are you that YOUR PARTNER will <u>not</u> be psychologically abusive toward you between now and the next time we meet?

1	2	3	4
Very certain	Fairly certain	Somewhat uncertain	Very uncertain

3. How certain are you that YOU will <u>not</u> be physically violent toward your partner between now and the next time we meet?

1	2	3	4
Very certain	Fairly certain	Somewhat uncertain	Very uncertain

4. How certain are you that YOU will <u>not</u> be psychologically abusive toward your partner between now and the next time we meet?

1	2	3	4
Very certain	Fairly certain	Somewhat uncertain	Very uncertain

2. We have altered the typical structure of couples therapy and begin and end each session by meeting separately with the male and female partners to determine whether conjoint work is safe or the risk of allowing any couple to leave the session together is too great. We describe this process in more detail later in the chapter.

3. During the postsession meeting, we ask each client to complete the end-of-session check sheet, and the therapists review the sheet before the client leaves (see Exhibit 10.1).

4. Although this program is couple-based, we reserve the flexibility to cancel the conjoint portion of the program and meet in separate-gender groups when necessary. Alternatively, one therapist may also meet individually with a couple or a partner to manage risk if this appears to be the best course of action.

5. Conjoint treatment may be terminated if, once it has begun, we determine that it is dangerous to continue. The client should be given referral options if conjoint therapy appears to increase the risk of continued violence.

6. Although the focus of DVFCT is on abuse, we also manage other mental health issues as they arise. Some clients may present with depression, anxiety, posttraumatic stress disorder, suicidal thoughts, or any number of other symptoms during the course of DVFCT. We intervene directly in these cases when it appears we can adequately provide treatment and refer to outside providers if not. At times, we may decide to suspend conjoint treatment if other psychological issues jeopardize the safety or usefulness of the conjoint work.

TREATMENT FORMAT FOR SESSIONS 7 THROUGH 18

We use a particular format for therapy sessions during the conjoint phase of treatment. Every session of the conjoint phase follows this format. We have found that this format allows us to anticipate and manage many potentially difficult situations that might otherwise lead to further aggression. This structure provides separate check-in time with partners before and after each session to monitor for violence and the risk of violence and to "decompress" after the conjoint portion of the session. Although this structure serves the same purpose in both the group and individual formats of the program, it is managed somewhat differently in each. In the following section, we describe the session structure and any differences in how it works for individual couples and for the multicouple group. The times suggested are approximate and may need to be changed depending on what is reported in each component of the session.

Presession Check-In (15–20 Minutes)

Each session in the conjoint phase begins with an individual check-in. In the group format, one cotherapist meets with the men separately and one with the women. For individual couples, the cotherapists each meet alone with one partner. In both formats, we systematically vary which cotherapist meets with which partner or group of partners from week to week so that the therapists do not become identified as the "men's therapist" or the "women's therapist." Regardless of whether we are meeting with an individual client or a men's or women's group, we begin the check-in with a 10-minute period of meditation using the procedure described in Chapter 7. If an individual or couple comes late to the session, we have one of the therapists meet with them separately for meditation before they join the ongoing session. We have found that the meditation period often allows clients to become centered before they begin conjoint work and also serves as a kind of psychological boundary between the stress of getting to the session and the actual session itself. Both therapists and clients are able to become more fully present in the session when we begin with a period of meditation. Next, we believe that it is important to begin by asking about risk and successes in the past week. To do so, we use the process we described in the chapter on Session 3. We begin with questions about successes in the past week and then move to questions about trouble spots and potential areas of risk or recurrence of violence. When participants report a new episode of aggression or increased risk, we ask if they feel safe talking about the incident with their partner present. This information is important in determining whether conjoint work should proceed that week. We next use a scaling question anchored in the miracle question or the Healthy Relationship House exercise to help clients gauge where they are currently. Reports of moving higher on the scale are met with questions that highlight how the clients were able to make that happen, whereas reports of staying the same or regressing are followed by efforts to understand how the clients kept difficult situations from becoming even worse. When such questions are asked genuinely, they help clients reflect on their own abilities to deal with difficulty. It is important, however, to empathize with the disappointment or discouragement that clients feel under such circumstances without inviting them to focus solely on the "failure" aspects of the week. We also find it important to ask clients what leads them to put themselves at any point on the scale. We find that often the most recent events (e.g., an argument in the car on the way to the session) tend to color a couple's views of the recent past. While we want to know about immediate difficulties, it is also helpful to ask the clients to extend their view back over the week to get a more complete picture. Questions such as the following can be helpful in this regard: "If you had rated your week before you and your partner got into an argument today, where would you have put yourself on the scale?" The effort here is not to "prove" to the client that things are better than he or she thinks but to try to help the client see a more complete picture. If the couple or either partner cannot report positive experiences, do not argue with them.

In addition to assessing successes, safety, and risk, the presession check-in also serves another purpose during the conjoint couples phase of treatment. It allows the therapists to begin to assess and plan for the actual conjoint work to take place in that session. The presession check-in provides a time for the therapists to ask the clients individually what issues they might like to raise in the conjoint part of the session. Sometimes, these issues will emerge from the discussion of success and safety described earlier. At other times, the clients may wish to raise other issues—issues not related directly to the events of the week. In our experience, such things as parenting difficulties, how to manage money and spending, relationships with extended family members, and other issues common to couples regardless of the presence of physical or emotional abuse are typical topics of discussion.

Therapist Check-In (5 Minutes)

After the presession client check-in, the therapists meet briefly to check in with each other and determine whether the plan for the session is still appropriate. The first order of business is to compare what has been reported in the separate sessions as a way to assess risk. If both partners report no physical or emotional aggression during the previous week, or if the reports of a new incident are consistent and the partners are not afraid to discuss the situation with each other, conjoint treatment can proceed. If one partner reports a new incident of physical aggression or severe conflict in the presession but the other partner does not report it, or if the reports differ significantly, we may consider not meeting with the couple conjointly, at least until other data have been gathered. We become even more reluctant to meet together if either partner reports being afraid of talking about the incident when they are together. Under those circumstances, we may meet separately to manage risk in the individual couple condition. In the multicouple group condition, we may assign one cotherapist to meet individually with the couple or with each partner separately to manage risk while the other cotherapist convenes the rest of the couples for the group session.

A second purpose of the therapist check-in is to develop a tentative agenda for the conjoint phase of the session if safety concerns do not preclude such a meeting. We describe this process in detail later for the multicouple group format because it entails a more complex process. For the individual couple condition, the therapists simply advise each other of any specific issues that either partner has indicated he or she wishes to raise. A tentative plan can be developed for how to address the issues of concern to the clients with the clear understanding that therapy sessions are not agenda-driven meetings and that flexibility is needed as nuances of the issues arise and need attention.

Conjoint Session (55 Minutes)

This portion of the session should include all clients and therapists unless a different plan was developed during the pretreatment check-in.

Postsession Separate-Gender Session (15 Minutes)

At the end of each session, we again meet separately with each partner—either individually or in men's group and women's groups as described earlier. This meeting serves two purposes. First, it gives the therapists time to determine whether all clients are safe to leave the session. At times, a participant will appear calm during the conjoint meeting but report being angry, resentful, agitated, or otherwise unsafe during the postsession check-in. If this is the case, we take a variety of actions to help the couple remain safe. We may remind clients of their own safety plan designed to protect their family members and ask which parts of it might be of help to them at this point. Some questions we have found useful are:

- "How do you usually manage to cool off when you are upset with your partner?"
- "What signs will you see that tell you your anger is under control?"
- "How will you feel best about dealing with the things you are feeling now?"

Further, we might give the client the chance to air his or her grievance about what just happened in the session with the promise that this can be added to the agenda for future work with the partner. We might even bring the couple together briefly and advise them not to discuss the issues that were brought up in the session until they meet again for therapy or until at least a day or two has passed. If the situation appears to be more imminently dangerous, we may arrange for the partners to leave separately and not to spend the evening together.

Although we have, on occasion, had to make such arrangements with clients to manage risk that has arisen in the session, we also find that the structure of the postsession meeting itself serves a protective function. Having the couple separate and meet in a different configuration and often a different room seems to have the effect of creating a boundary between the conjoint work and their return home. This simple change in context can often allow participants to see their recent interactions from a different vantage point, one with less rancor. The postsession meeting can serve as something of a "mini time out," a time for each partner to reflect on his or her emotional state and vulnerability to violence or relationship conflict.

In addition to verbally assessing risk, partners are also asked to complete individually two short questionnaires about their perception of the helpfulness of the session and their feelings of immediate safety (Exhibit 10.1 and Exhibit 10.2). Therapists review the feedback on the helpfulness of the session each week. In addition, as we noted in the chapter on assessment, we try to rely on multiple modalities for collecting data about safety and risk. Four scaling questions are used to assess the extent to which clients are convinced that they or their partner will not be physically or psychologically abusive during the following week. The therapists review the clients' answers to these questions and follow up on any indications of risk or fear using the same strategies described earlier.

EXHIBIT 10.2
Weekly Session Evaluation

1. How helpful was this session? (Circle the number below that best describes the degree to which this session was helpful to you).

NOT HELPFUL AT ALL							EXTREMELY HELPFUL
	1	2	3	4	5	6	

2. What happened during the session that was not very useful?

_____

_____

3. What happened that was useful?

_____

_____

4. Circle all the things below that the <u>counselors</u> could have done differently to improve the usefulness of this session for you.

Talk less   Talk more   Be more supportive of me   Be less supportive of me

Be more supportive of my partner   Be less supportive of my partner   Nothing

Something but I don't know what   Other _____

5. Circle all the things that <u>you</u> could have done differently to make this session more useful for you.

Talk less   Talk more   Listen more attentively   Be less defensive

Get more involved   Trust more   Keep my sense of humor   Think more

Be more honest about things   Other _____

6. Circle all the words that best describe how you felt during today's session.

Safe   Anxious   Depressed   Involved   Bored   Angry   Content

Tense   Understood   Pleased   Detached   Worthless   Comfortable

Important   Scared   Other _____

Although the primary purpose of this structure is to assess and manage risk, another outcome in the multicouple group format is to increase bonding among the male and female members of the group separately. As the relationships develop in the same-gender groups, ideally they enable the clients to begin giving one another direct and honest feedback. The separate pregroup meetings also provide a forum for clients to raise difficult issues and hear responses from the group and the leaders without raising those issues with their partners present. At times, this serves as a kind of rehearsal for later raising touchy issues in the conjoint group. At other times, it allows clients to discuss issues they are as yet unwilling to raise with their partner present but that they need to discuss and get help with. One female client told us:

> [The separate groups are] helpful because it is supportive for the women. When we go into the class with the guys and the women together, and I have had a hard week with my husband and we've yelled and he's thrown things around the house and he's done all this stuff, I can't really talk to anybody because I'm afraid that he is going to do something. So by going in and talking to the women first it kind of gets it off my chest.

THE CONJOINT SESSION

We would like to be able to provide a step-by-step road map to guide clinicians through a conjoint session in DVFCT. Such a road map, however, would misrepresent the process, not unlike how a real road map can only give the barest outline of what the actual journey will entail. Solution-focused brief therapy (SFBT; e.g., de Shazer et al., 2007), the model underlying our work, takes as its premise attending to the specific goals and needs of the clients sitting in the room with you rather a preconceived notion of how therapy should progress. One of the axioms of SFBT is that there are many paths to a solution—meaning that people find many ways to reach a state of affairs that they find satisfactory. Within broad limits, SFBT asks that therapists not prejudge the particular solution at which a client arrives. Even though we ask the multicouple group members in Session 2 to arrive at a collective vision of a healthy relationship in the Healthy Relationship House exercise, a given couple may find that parts of the vision fit them and parts do not. For some couples, for instance, closeness may involve talking regularly about issues that are important to them, whereas other couples may experience closeness primarily through shared activities or through the joys and struggles of parenting. Each couple in DVFCT arrives at their own relationship destination, the worth of which is judged primarily by the degree to which it suits both partners.

Although this stance provides a great deal of respect for the wishes of our clients and freedom for them to choose their own path, it does not give therapists much concrete guidance. As much as we would like to say that we ask a scaling question whenever a client reports feeling better or that we always ask coping questions when couples report being stalled in their progress, we do not. In SFBT, one size does not fit all. In fact, any intervention may fit one situation today and not be appropriate for a similar situation tomorrow. With this in mind, we have decided to elucidate a set of principles that we rely on in our work with couples in the conjoint phase of treatment, along with some of the techniques or interventions that can operationalize them. We believe that these principles provide a sound structure for our work. Their application also demands creativity and flexibility from the therapists, something that we have found keeps our work alive and stimulating. We should note that a complete discussion of the SFBT model is beyond the scope of this work. The Suggested Readings section contains a list of resources that will help readers delve more deeply into SFBT, which we recommend for practitioners who wish to deliver the DVFCT model but do not have a strong background in SFBT.

The following subsections describe the principles we find useful in doing this work.

Questions as Primary Tools

All therapy approaches use questions, of course. However, in SFBT, asking questions serves as the primary conversational stance of the therapists (de Shazer et al., 2007). Questions invite the clients' own thoughts, approaches, resources, and hopes to have precedence in the therapeutic work. To this end, questions should be as genuine as possible and should not be disguised attempts to teach or convey information or otherwise elicit from the client information the therapist thinks is important. "What are the qualities of a healthy relationship for you two as a couple?" is quite different from asking, "How are you going to develop respect in your relationship?" when the clients have not explicitly said they feel respect is important to them. Although any of us might assume that respect is an important part of a strong relationship, it is up to the clients rather than the therapists to decide this. A number of kinds of questions are somewhat unique to SFBT, as described next.

The Miracle Question

The *miracle question* is a process for generating a future vision and, it is hoped, helping clients rise above the seemingly inviolable constraints in which they see their situation. We described this approach in detail in Chapter 5. Although we first use the miracle question in Session 2 of Phase 1, it can be used again at any time during Phase 2 when orienting the couple toward the future and the absence of the problem might be useful.

Exception Questions

Exception questions draw attention to times when the problem did not happen or when it was less severe. One of the foundational assumptions of SFBT is that change is always happening. Clients—and often therapists—talk about problems as if they are constant and unchanging. Doing so obscures the fact that there are variations in problem situations. Sometimes a difficult conversation does not lead to conflict. Depressed moods ebb and flow. Exception questions point to these variations and bring them into focus. In Phase 2, for instance, the therapists may ask couples to talk about times when they managed conflict successfully, when they expressed affection to each other if this is not a common occurrence, or when they spent time together without arguing. Paying attention to these exceptions draws attention to islands of good functioning in what may seem like a sea of troubles and can point to resources the couple can use to change and also provide hope that change is ultimately possible. Finding exceptions also sets the stage for the next kind of question we discuss—agency questions.

Agency Questions

Agency questions increase the client's sense of agency or influence over events that are exceptions to an established problem. It is often tempting for clients to dismiss exceptions as anomalies that are out of their control. Agency questions, therefore, ask the clients to reflect on how they contributed to the exception occurring. Agency questions can be as simple as "How did you do that?" or "What part did you play in that happening?" Sometimes humor can be helpful: "Now tell me, were you there when you and your wife had a good talk? . . . So, if you were there, you must have had something to do with it? What was it?" Any question that invites clients to take responsibility for their own progress or success can be considered an agency question.

Scaling Questions

Scaling questions are a mainstay of SFBT work. A typical scaling question uses a range of 0 to 10 where 0 is anchored in a time when the problem was prominent in the life of the client (0 = When you knew you were going to start this program is an anchor we often use) and 10 is anchored to a time when the problem has been eliminated or has receded in importance (10 = The day after the miracle). Scaling questions serve a variety of purposes. First, they allow the client and therapist to quickly evaluate progress toward sometimes large and difficult-to-grasp outcomes (e.g. "a healthy relationship"). Scaling questions also put determining progress and direction in the hands of the client. It is the client, after all, not the therapist, who selects the number on the scale that reflects the progress made. In addition, scaling questions imply a series of steps in any change effort—a suggestion that can provide a realistic view for the client and also point to next steps. If a client reports being at a 4 on the scale, it is logical, for instance, to ask what next steps would take her to a 4.5.

An Eye for Successes

Throughout the course of DVFCT in general, and Phase 2 specifically, the therapists keep listening for experiences of success that can be noticed and highlighted. Often, if the therapists do not underline successes, they may easily pass unnoticed, and the possibilities for more widespread change they hold can be lost. Clients often miss experiences of success because they have become mired in a view of their situation that is dominated by problems. When you are starving for something to eat, you are less likely to notice the lovely view of the mountains from the road that you are frantically driving down in search of a restaurant. There is even evidence accumulating from the field of neuroscience suggesting that humans are shaped by evolution to notice problems more readily than successes (Hanson, 2009). Intentional efforts are needed to take in good experiences. When therapists hear about successes, they need to slow the conversation down and ask about them. This does two things. It helps the couple notice the successes that may serve as building blocks for further progress and it educates the couple that successes are worthy of notice and discussion in DVFCT. The intention to focus on success in SFBT has sometimes been misinterpreted as a prohibition against talking about problems or difficulties. Nothing could be further from the truth. People need to talk about the suffering that brought them to therapy, and if therapists try to suppress that expression, clients will not feel heard, nor will they trust that their therapist truly understands enough to help. What distinguishes SFBT from some other approaches to therapy is that SFBT therapists do not necessarily elicit discussions of problems nor purposefully prolong or elaborate on them. Thus, although clients often talk about difficult issues in SFBT, therapists using this model would be less likely to ask questions to gather more and more details about what is not working. Instead, they would listen carefully for areas of better functioning and try to help the client balance the picture by remarking on those areas as well as the less helpful ones.

Orienting to the Future

A basic tenet of SFBT is that the future is both negotiable and created (Pichot & Dolan, 2003). That is, the steps that clients take in the present lead them to where they find themselves in the future. Therefore, we feel that it is important to keep a clear vision of the clients' desired outcomes in the forefront of treatment. Failure to do so can result in missing the mark. As described earlier, we use the miracle question for individual couples, and the Healthy Relationship House exercise in the multicouple group, to help couples develop a specific vision of the outcome they wish to reach. Once our clients have a clearer vision, we then anchor the current work they are doing in the context of progress toward that vision through the regular use of inquiry, including scaling questions. Beginning in Session 3, we regularly use a scaling question based on the miracle question or the Healthy Relationship House exercise during the initial check-in. Doing so gauges progress and orients clients to thinking about the outcome they are seeking as a result of therapy. At the end of sessions, we often ask clients what actions on their part might move them slightly closer to their desired outcome. This, too, can be done with the use of a scaling question. For instance, if a client began the session by saying she was at a 4, we might ask, "What would you be willing to do, if anything, before our next meeting that would move you to a 4.5?"

Although we continue throughout the course of DVFCT to anchor our work in a vision of the future, we also know that goal setting is a process and not just an event. It is rare for clients to be pursuing the exact miracle at the end of treatment that they defined in Session 2. Nor should we expect them to. Like everything, desired outcomes have fluidity and evolve in the context of new experiences. Small successes may help clients attempt bigger and more far-reaching goals as their confidence in their ability to change increases. However, confrontation with the realities of their situation may force a complete shift in direction. Slavish adherence to goals set at the beginning of treatment can hamper the creativity that is a hallmark of SFBT.

When Something Works, Make It Bigger

Allied with our continual effort to notice successes is the idea that small changes contain the germ of larger changes. Therefore, when couples report to us that something they have done has had a positive effect, we try to help them find ways to enlarge the influence of that success. This process uses some of the techniques already described. Agency questions are especially useful because clients often downplay or fail to recognize the part they have played in a success. Without taking responsibility for positive changes, they are left feeling that the experience was a fluke and not reproducible. Clients can also be asked to project the influence of a small change into the future. For a couple who report that they are listening to each other more calmly and without immediately challenging the other's views, we might ask, "Suppose you were able to keep doing this consistently. If you did, what might be different in your relationship in 3 months? What do you think you would each notice that was different?"

Making positive occurrences bigger has at least two benefits for therapists working with couples that have experienced violence. First, noticing small positive changes can be a source of hope for discouraged couples. Many of our clients come to us saying that DVFCT is their last hope. More than once we've heard, "If this doesn't help us, we're going to get divorced." Seeing small changes and having the therapists and group members in the multicouple group format validate those changes can be meaningful to clients. A second benefit of making successes bigger is that unlike other approaches to therapy, it does not focus on clients doing new things. It asks them to do more of what is already working. One problem with skill training approaches to therapy is that they depend on clients learning a series of new behaviors. This requires focused effort and motivation. For couples whose hope for change is low, SFBT offers an alternative: Simply learn to do more of the things that are working. This often appears to be a much less formidable task than doing something new. The following transcript from the end of a multicouple group session illustrates the therapist's intentional efforts to emphasize and enlarge a couple's report of a successful conversation:

Therapist: I'd like you to stay another 5 minutes. I'd like to end on a positive note. Can people do that? Because [Female Client], you said something in the presession that I thought was really worth sharing with everybody, and that was the reason that you guys were late. One of you want to share it again?

Male Client: She better, because I'll say something different.

Female Client: It can be said differently, then that's understood. I just said we were late because we had time before to have some dinner and sort of our own little meeting, and we were talking and relating like we hadn't related in a long time, communicating not necessarily about negative things but positive things, and it was very nice, and I didn't want to leave. And [Male Client] kept saying, "We've got to go; we're going to be late." And I was like, "No." You know, I wasn't ready, because we needed to finish where we were, and I felt like that was a part of what this is about, that we could talk and communicate in a way without a formality or without anyone else being there, and that was a very nice feeling, and it still is.

Therapist: And I'm wondering, I guess, how did you guys accomplish that? I mean, how did you make that happen? What did you do to be able to be able to sit down with just the two of you and do it? 'Cause that's our ultimate goal; we don't want you to keep coming here.

Male Client: Well, I think the key thing is the positive, even if you're talking about negative things, using positive vocabulary.

Therapist: OK.

Female Client: But we were relaxed, and I think that has a [lot] to do with it.

Male Client: Time is important.

Female Client: We were almost dating. I mean, I think it was sort of like that, you know. It was like a date for me . . .

Male Client: Well, actually we were . . .

Female Client: It was relaxed.

Male Client:	We were talking about her parents and why did I feel uncomfortable, and I said, "They're very loving people; I just wasn't raised in that style, you know." That's why it was uncomfortable for me. It wasn't that her parents were bad people. It's just . . .
Therapist:	Well, I got the impression that this was a conversation that you could have had in the past, and it could have gone much differently.
Male Client:	Oh, it could have been ballistic!
Therapist:	OK, so what did you do different this time that allowed you to have and for it to be a relaxed conversation? Here's a conversation that could have been ballistic, but you guys had it in a relaxed fashion. It was almost a date! You know . . .
Female Client:	We were at dinner.
Therapist:	You guys did something very different or something very well to make that happen.
Male Client:	Well, I think all the conversations were in a positive mode, I mean.
Female Client:	There were no children; we were not in our own home setting.
Male Client:	That all helps.
Therapist:	OK, so get rid of the distractions.
Female Client:	There was nothing else to fidget with.
Therapist:	What else?
Male Client:	Also, we said this was nice and we're going to continue to . . . Remember, I said, "We have these meetings to thank for having a night off, because we've set everything aside, and we have babysitters. Keep continuing to do this, whether we have a meeting or not. It's very important to take the time off." We had a good weekend too, with the kids, but, you know, just taking time off!
Therapist:	What kind of tools did you guys use to actually make the conversation successful?
Female Client:	There was no—I don't think there was any stress. I mean, it wasn't aimed at one person. I guess it was, um . . .

Therapist:	So, it was more about the issue than about . . . It didn't get at personalities in the relationship. It just got straight to the issue. Is that accurate?
Female Client:	Yeah, but there—it didn't seem like—it was more flowing. It wasn't like, "Well, these are some topics we have, and this is what we're going to talk about." It flowed in from one thing to the other and other relationships we had in the past, how they were successful, and that was interesting.
Therapist:	So, you were looking for strengths, things that worked before.
Male Client:	Well, actually, yeah, we've just . . . We're having good conversations. I'm surprised at how long we've been together, how we're actually setting up different goals—you know, mutual goals, accomplishing things. I mean, a mutual goal is to take time off at the same time.
Therapist:	So, you're acknowledging some progress.
Female Client:	Yeah, because—go on.
Male Client:	Yeah, well, also this thing about children; who is going to take care of the kids and also trying to figure out times when we can be together and do something exciting with the children, instead of shuffling them back and forth.
Female Client:	Like, the big test is this vacation going on for a week, and we've talked about having a child care provider come with us for part of it, and then we decided, "No, we have enough of that here, so let's just try to let our hair down and have fun with our kids who just probably really need us to have fun with them." But that's going to be a real test, because it is stressful, no matter whether you're having fun with them or not. Children become stressful sometimes.
Therapist:	Um, last thing, then we gotta go, but I just wanted—a couple things that I heard both of you say. One: Picking a time was important, That there was, without the distractions, less stress, without the kids around, to sit and be able to do it, to have fun doing it. You stuck to the issue, instead of getting off on personalities or the relationship. Talking about the things you're doing well, not just what was the issue. Now, last question: What does it tell you—I mean, the fact that you were able to do this

	so well; what does that say to you? What does that tell you about your relationship?
Female Client:	Well, I hope that we can continue to do that well at times.
Therapist:	You're dodging my question.
Female Client:	What? Well, I guess I am. What does that tell us—
Therapist:	What did it mean to you, that you were able to sit down and do this?
Female Client:	For me, that we have a friendship and that we have something special.
Male Client:	Yeah, it meant that the uh—there was no static. It was, uh, there could be smooth sailing somewhere over the horizon, way over the horizon.
Therapist:	So, for you there was—it meant hope that things could go well.
Male Client:	Well, I think we've—it's unbelievable; we've had it—We felt very, very well to have moved into this house, which, you know, could be the most stressful thing in the world, but it's been great.
Therapist:	All right. Thank you all.

Make It Interactional

Because we are dealing with couples, our focus is not simply on two partners in isolation from one another. We are also interested in the interactional changes they are making. Two principles guide us here: looking for solution sequences and projecting interactional change into the future.

Solution Sequences

Elsewhere, we have written about the concept of problem and solution sequences (McCollum & Trepper, 2001). Briefly, problem behavior can be seen as occurring as part of a predictable pattern of interaction in families, a concept taken from the strategic school of therapy (Haley, 1976). Changing the pattern or sequence early in the process will result in a change in behavior later in the process. With careful questioning, a couple can be helped to define the typical pattern that leads them into conflict. We have modified this concept somewhat to think in terms of *solution sequences*—that is, the sequence or pattern of behavior that results in successes or exceptions. When a couple reports that things have gone well—especially when it is a situation in which they might have gone badly—we ask a series of questions to help the couple define the solution sequence. We are specifically interested in what each partner contributed at each step along the way to lead to a good outcome. We usually begin by enlarging the success and making sure it is noticed using strategies described earlier. We find it especially important to make positive changes interactional when the couple defines them as individual achievements. We start the process by asking each partner where they were and what they were doing when the success occurred. We then trace the sequence of events leading up to the success and what each partner contributed to make it possible. At times, a partner's contribution to success may be refraining from doing something rather than acting. Regularly, when asked what their contribution to a success was, clients will say, "Nothing. I didn't do anything." We then ask what they might have done in the past when a similar situation didn't go as well, and we hear things such as, "I would have told him to shut up," or "I would have reminded her of all the times I did help around the house." This allows us to make the point that doing "nothing" is really doing something to improve the quality of the relationship in certain circumstances.

Making change interactional serves the purpose of keeping both partners involved in the change effort. If the focus is solely on individual efforts, one partner may come to bear more responsibility for change. At the same time, there is a need for balance. If the focus is solely on interactional issues, personal responsibility, which is a foundation of DVFCT, can get lost as well. We believe that the two issues are in a dynamic relationship with one another. In any situation, individuals bear the responsibility of making the best choices they can of the ones available to them. Thus, even if a wife slaps her husband, he has the responsibility for choosing among the reactions available to him; we see striking her back, for instance, as a choice, not an inevitable reaction. At the same time, the relational context may shape or limit the alternatives available. If a woman refuses to participate in a time out called by her male partner and blocks his way as he tries to leave the room, he then has to choose what to do from a limited number of alternatives. Nothing absolves him of the responsibility to make the best choice available to him, however. In our view, the best choice is the nonviolent choice.

Future-Oriented Interactional Questions

Whereas solution sequences focus on bringing successes from the past into the present, future-oriented interactional questions project current positive changes into the future. This technique asks clients to imagine what their lives would be like if the positive changes in the present continue to build over time. We usually begin with questions about the near future. Such a conversation with a couple after they had reported having a calm discussion about a conflictual parenting issue might go something like this:

Therapist to Female Partner:	Amanda, if your husband was able to talk more calmly to you about how to deal with Phillip, what reaction would he see back from you?
Amanda:	I think I would take a minute to think about what he was saying and maybe take it more seriously than when he is screaming at me.
Therapist to Male Partner:	Paul, if Amanda took what you were saying more seriously, what would she see back from you?
Paul:	Maybe I wouldn't get so afraid she was just blowing me off like she does. When she does that, it really makes me mad. If she would take me seriously, I think I would want to know what she thought we should do. I'd like us to be in this parenting thing together.

As this bit of dialogue illustrates, the first step is to project small changes into the immediate future. As couples make more progress, however, they may begin to report dramatic changes in their interaction—changes that are more global. It is useful to project these changes into the future as well.

Therapist:	So you two have had several good weeks now. You're talking regularly and without tension. You're even having some fun times together. Suppose those changes keep growing over the next 6 months. What do you think would be going on in your lives then?
Wife:	I think maybe we might take a vacation. The last time we took a vacation we fought the whole time and all I wanted to do was come home. After that, I never wanted to go away with him again. But if things keep going like this, maybe we could go away again, maybe even without the kids.

Just as the miracle question and the Healthy Relationship House give couples a beginning definition of their desired future, future-oriented relational questions continue to refine and concretize that vision and serve to maintain motivation to continue the work of changing their relationship.

Have a Sense of Humor

Although therapy is important work, it becomes stagnant without a measure of playfulness and humor. Of course, we are not suggesting that jokes be made at the client's expense but simply that therapists respond genuinely when clients express or demonstrate some of the absurdity of life that we all experience. In our research study, several clients emphasized the importance of humor. One male client said:

> Don't take away humor. Because if you can laugh at a situation, then you're not going to go and get angry. There's been a lot of humor. You have to learn laughter is the best medicine. That's the truth. It's a very good way to learn to deal with something.

Believe in the Client's Positive Intentions

The men and women in this program have agreed to participate in couples therapy because they want to remain together. All of the clients have agreed that they want to end the violence in their relationships. Although it is always tempting as outsiders to look at others' lives in terms of what they are doing wrong and what we might do differently, this is not a helpful attitude for therapists. We believe that people bring what strengths they have to life; the therapist's job is to help clients recognize and build on those strengths and to make changes in things that are not going well for them. A moralistic approach to people's problems impedes joining and makes therapy much harder for the therapist and less useful for the client. The use of *presuppositional questions*, which presume that clients have positive intentions and that change is likely, are important. Examples of presuppositional questions include the following:

- "How *will* things be different *when* violence is no longer a part of your relationship?"
- "What *will* you be doing with your time *when* you do not have to put so much energy into avoiding conflict?"

Use the Client's Language and Metaphors

At times it can be helpful to use the client's own language or metaphors. We have found that speaking the client's language gives the therapist more believability as long as it is done authentically. Nothing is less believable than someone pretending to be what they're not—especially when there are cultural or ethnic differences between the therapist and the client. However, when you can wholeheartedly use a metaphor or language you share with a client, the effect can be powerful. If you do not know the client's world and cannot speak his or her language, do not try to fake it. A better strategy is to ask questions and to gather information. Nothing empowers clients more than letting them teach you about something they know.

Use Compliments

Clients are often surprised to come to therapy and receive a compliment from their therapist. However, a compliment serves as a concrete way to let clients know that the therapist is interested not only in hearing the story of what's gone wrong but in looking for positive aspects of their life as well. Most of us feel more relaxed and open interpersonally when others in a relationship communicate that they're "on our side." Sometimes something the client says or does in the therapy session will lead to a compliment.

At the very least, therapists can compliment clients for coming to couples treatment. You can certainly compliment your client on being open-minded enough to come to see whether therapy has anything to offer. By the same token, do not be unrealistic or patronizing with your compliments. False praise does not feel like much of a compliment.

Acknowledge Clients' Pain

Solution-focused therapy is not an emotionally distant process in which the therapist tries to figure out intellectually elegant solutions to problems. Clients come to us with real and painful problems. It is often important to them to know that we understand their pain before they will trust us enough to help them look elsewhere for strengths and solutions. Doing so is a sometimes tricky process because it is important that you acknowledge the client's dilemmas and suffering while not becoming involved in the hopelessness of the client's view.

Practice and Model Metadialogue

One way in which the cotherapy team can work together is to dialogue with one another in the presence of the couple. The couple is asked to listen and not respond immediately to what the cotherapists discuss. Metadialogues allow cotherapists to comment on the couple's process, deescalate rising conflict in the session, explore and challenge gender-role stereotypes, shift the couple's focus from problems to strengths, model alternative conflict resolution skills, and introduce difficult material without directly challenging the couple (for a more complete discussion of methodologies see Tucker, Stith, Howell, McCollum, & Rosen, 2000). The metadialogue invites the couple to step outside their constricted view of themselves and their relationship for a moment and consider other ways of seeing the situation. During a metadialogue, the cotherapists can present several competing views of what the couple is experiencing without directly endorsing any of them. The therapists can also express their own multiple or conflicting views—for example, a concern about the woman's safety and empathy for the pain she has experienced can be juxtaposed to the wish to support the man as he struggles to accept responsibility for his past acts of violence and to prevent future ones. Finally, the cotherapists can adopt a respectful, not-knowing stance that does not foreclose reality through the therapists' pronouncement of "what is" but encourages fluidity and possibility through the therapists' reflection about "what might be." By including the reflective stance within a solution-focused model, the therapists are able to use wider, multiple lenses that help avoid the limiting, simplistic views that can alienate clients (Meth, 1992), and the couple benefits from seeing their situation from different angles and new perspectives.

Look for the Success Inside the "Failure"

Asking clients how they would like their lives to be different and helping them see which parts of that dream are already happening and can be expanded on are only part of the story. Clients also need to be helped to deal with the inevitable difficulties that arise throughout the course of therapy. Setbacks are particularly discouraging to clients early in the process, when they have only a little faith that they can make the changes they wish to make. We therefore try to look for signs of success even when it appears as though clients have "failed" in some way.

When clients experience a difficult time, the first order of business is to assess risk and make sure that safety has not been compromised. If risk is high or safety is an issue, steps need to be taken immediately. Most of the time, however, we find that couples come in after a week or two of improvement and report another fight that, although not increasing danger, has left them feeling that they are back where they started and have not made any progress. The first strategy in this circumstance is to empathize with how difficult change is and how discouraging it is when it seems like things have fallen apart, especially after a period of calm. If we try to move too quickly in looking for the successful elements of what happened, clients will feel dismissed or patronized in their concern. Once we have understood the anguish involved in the situation, we begin to turn the focus to things that might have gone right. Few situations are completely negative. Figure 10.1 illustrates a process for finding the successes inside seeming failures.

Once safety has been assessed and we have noticed and empathized with the sense of discouragement that is expectable following a setback, we proceed to do our best to assess what happened realistically. Often, setbacks are described in global and absolute terms as evidence that no progress has been made and that there is no reason to have any hope about the future. Although this may represent the couple's emotional understanding of the situation, it

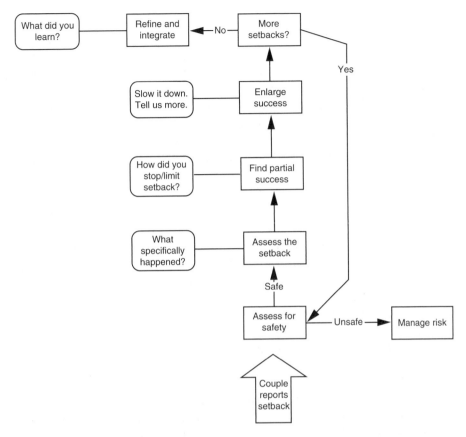

Figure 10.1. Process for finding success inside seeming failure in domestic violence–focused couples therapy.

may not represent the actuality of what has happened. Asking for specific behavioral descriptions of what happened can begin to yield a more balanced view. A couple presenting with a recurrence of marital conflict, for instance, might first be asked on what day the argument happened. One couple told us about a difficult argument they had after the husband overdrew their checking account. He had a history of substance abuse problems, and financial chaos had been a continuing difficulty for the family when he was actively using. His wife became immediately suspicious that he had relapsed despite a lack of evidence that this was so. He tried to explain to her that he had simply misunderstood the amount of money in their account when he wrote a check and that he would transfer money from another account to cover the overdraft. This led to further accusations and blame about the ongoing financial problems the couple faced. Their argument had consumed nearly an hour of open conflict and then several hours of isolation from each other before they had reached an uneasy peace that lasted for another day until they came to therapy. We began by empathizing with how frightening it was for the wife to think that they might be returning to the chaotic life they lived when her husband was actively using, and we empathized with the husband about how difficult it was to not be trusted by his wife. It was important for us not to enter into an effort to determine whether the client had actually relapsed. Our focus was on how the couple had handled this situation interactionally. On the basis of their description of what actually happened, we were able to point out to them that the heightened conflict had lasted for about 2 days. Even while they were more distant from one another, they had managed to get their children to school and day care, and both had gone to work. Furthermore, although there had been arguing and raised voices, neither one had assaulted the other, nor had there been the threats of divorce and taking away the children that had happened in the past. They had also used their negotiated time-out plan and made a decision to discuss the issue in therapy when they determined that neither was capable of a productive discussion. Thus, we were able to find several partial successes in their description of what happened. Had we left the description at the global level, we would not have known about the partial successes.

As we began to notice and comment on the partial successes, the couple tended to minimize them. For instance, when we talked about their successful use of time out to manage a difficult situation, the husband said, "Well, we didn't have a choice. It had gotten to that point." We then began to ask detailed questions about how they had decided to use time out. How had they remembered to do so? Who made the suggestion to use it? How had the other partner agreed to participate? Slowing down and getting more details about a partial success helps to draw the clients' attention to it and enlarge the influence of that success. As the partners began to consider the very real differences they were reporting between how they used to handle conflict and what had happened in the past week, the tone of their conversation shifted, and they began to feel some ownership of what they had accomplished. We asked a variety of questions to help them each explain the part they had played in not letting a potentially explosive conflict get out of hand. We asked if there had been other rough spots over the course of the week that needed attention, and they said no. In fact, they told us that it had been a particularly good week, with two calm and satisfying evenings spent at home with their children before the overdraft was discovered. This led to an even more realistic view of their setback—that it had been only 2 days, whereas in the past they had stayed angry at one another for days at a time. To help them integrate their new view of the situation, we asked them what they had learned that would help them the next time they encountered a difficult situation. They told us that they had learned that time out really did help them (they had been skeptical about it in the past) and that they could make it work to reduce the risk of aggression.

Although it might seem as though the focus on strengths and the future would leave clients feeling that we were not taking their concerns or situation seriously, we find this is not typically the case. One female client told us the following during an interview about her experience of the program:

> I just feel so safe, number one. So comfortable. I think I talk too much sometimes, but I just have so much to say. But I feel heard. I feel with the information they give me back, it's something I've looked for in other counselors, because I wanted something to go home to do. Something to work on. They asked for a vision, and that made me think, OK, I've got to get my visions. They asked for us to identify concrete things—how things worked so well this week. That would be something to work on, to identify these things to help us help ourselves by learning the patterns that work for us.

11

CONSTRAINTS, MULTICOUPLE GROUP ADAPTATIONS, AND TERMINATION

At times, therapists encounter constraints to solution-focused work, situations that we believe compel us to become more directive and thereby deviate from some of the principles of solution-focused work delineated in the previous chapter. In addition, there are aspects of using this model in the multicouple group format that we believe deserve particular attention. Finally, in domestic violence–focused couples therapy (DVFCT), the termination phase is particularly important because it lays the foundation for continuing safety and, it is hoped, sets the stage for more growth in relationship satisfaction. We discuss each of these issues in this chapter.

CONSTRAINTS TO SOLUTION-FOCUSED WORK

Not all the setbacks or situations that couples experience during the conjoint phase of DVFCT are amenable to intervention using the approach we have discussed in previous chapters. At times, setbacks include indications of increased risk of aggression or otherwise suggest that we need to shift out of our primary solution-focused approach to intervene more directly, a process discussed briefly in Chapter 3. The primary arenas for monitoring the need to step out of the solution-focused approach are the separate-gender meetings before and after the conjoint portion of the session. Although each case has to be judged individually, we have identified some general classes of constraints.

Enacting a Safety Plan

The primary concern, of course, is increased risk of violence. If the therapists have any reason to believe that there is increased risk, several courses of action are available. The first decision is whether it is safe to hold the conjoint portion of the meeting. If there has been a recent violent episode, or if the therapists believe there is imminent risk of violence, they should forgo the conjoint meeting in favor of active risk management. This may mean sending the couple home separately, helping them implement their safety plans developed in Session 4, planning a temporary separation, involving law enforcement personnel, or anything else needed to preserve each partner's safety.

Maria and Jorge came to group one night obviously upset. Both reported that they had had a major conflict over a decision about their son Sergio's school program. The school wanted to place Sergio in special reading classes. Jorge thought this was a good idea and would help Sergio make progress, but Maria was against it, thinking it would stigmatize their son, who was already a somewhat shy child who had difficulty making friends. For some time, they had had conflicts about what was best for their son, and this discussion quickly erupted into shouting and ended when Jorge sought to take a time out and Maria pursued him, still wanting to talk. She grabbed Jorge when he tried to leave the room, and he pushed her out of his way. Maria was tearful and said she was somewhat fearful about discussing the incident in the group that night, and Jorge reported that he was still quite angry and wasn't sure he could talk calmly. During the break before the conjoint meeting, the therapists decided not to include Maria and Jorge in the rest of group that night. Although each told the same story about the incident, its immediacy and the fact that both partners did not feel it would be advisable to discuss it in group that evening led to the therapists' decision. One therapist convened the rest of the couples for the conjoint phase while the other met with Maria and Jorge individually.

When she met with Maria, the therapist reminded her of the structure of the couple's time-out plan. Maria reported that she had panicked, thinking Jorge would leave and later call the school without consulting her to enroll Sergio in special classes. The therapist reminded Maria of the "time-in" process in negotiated time-out and that, if need be, the therapists could help them come back to this contentious issue. The therapist also revisited Maria's safety plan with her, reminding her that keeping herself safe meant using safety tools such as time out. The therapist also empathized with Maria's concerns about

Sergio and offered to put that issue on the agenda for the next group if Maria and Jorge had not come to some agreement by then. The therapist then met with Jorge, who said he was still upset. He was particularly angry that he had been trying to use time out and that, in his view, Maria had not abided by their agreement. When the therapist asked if he was safe to go home with Maria, he said he was afraid that more conflict would erupt and that he would be again be in the position of trying to leave and having to defend himself. With the therapist's help, Jorge decided it would be best to spend the night with his brother, who lived close by. While keeping them separate, the therapist served as an intermediary and told Maria about her husband's plan for the night. Maria agreed, with the provision that neither of them would contact the school about the special classes for Sergio until they had talked and were in agreement. The therapist suggested they not contact one another until the next day. Jorge agreed to this and left to stay with his brother while Maria remained a little longer to do some meditation practice with the therapist to calm down. Obviously, in this case, in which we felt there was little danger of Maria following Jorge to his brother's house, we brokered an agreement between the two. If we thought there was danger of one partner following the other and harming him or her, we would not share either partner's location with the other.

In our experience, interventions at this level have been rare. A much more typical scenario has been a situation that leads us to believe that a couple needs more directive intervention than would be typical in the solution-focused approach.

Addressing Psychiatric Conditions or Stressful Life Circumstances

As we described briefly in Chapter 3, we often find circumstances that present constraints to solution-focused work, situations in which we feel we need to intervene directly. An example may be helpful. One couple who participated in the multicouple group, Frank and Emma, were struggling with stepfamily issues. Frank's young-adult son, Adrian, was living with the couple and was the source of a great deal of friction that often erupted into bitter arguments, yelling and screaming, and, on one occasion, an episode of the Frank and Emma pushing and shoving each other. Adrian had a serious drug problem and had undergone several attempts at treatment, including a lengthy stay in a residential facility. Despite that, he continued to relapse, at times with life-threatening consequences. Over the course of treatment, Emma began to notice that Frank's anger at her increased whenever Adrian was having more signs of relapse and a return to drug use. It also appeared to us that Frank was becoming more depressed, and his mood made it difficult for him to see any positive movement in his relationship with Emma, even when there was evidence that she was doing some things differently. In this case, we determined that his depression and his concern about his son constituted a constraint to solution-focused treatment. We referred him for a psychiatric consultation to assess his depression and determine the usefulness of an antidepressant. Because his son's situation was of primary concern and because it was a topic that we felt would consume too much focus were it to be addressed in the group, one of us met individually with him periodically while Emma and the rest of the couples met in group. During our individual sessions with Frank, we talked about Adrian, what he could realistically do to help him, his sadness and guilt about his situation, and how it might be connected to Frank's anger with Emma. Over time, and with the addition of an antidepressant, Frank's mood began to improve, and he was able to better control his anger with Emma. At that point, we decided to discontinue the individual sessions, and Frank returned full time to the multicouple group.

Frank and Emma's case represents a situation in which there was no indication of imminent risk, but part of what was happening for the couple stood in the way of working from a solution-focused perspective in the multicouple group. Although each case has to be judged individually, we have identified some general classes of constraints.

Teaching Communication and Conflict-Resolution Skills

One of the most common constraints is skill deficits. Some couples simply lack the requisite skills to communicate clearly or to resolve conflicts effectively. Although we could wait for moments of better communication and then do our best to expand them, in a time-limited program like DVFCT, we often include a brief psychoeducational component if necessary. We still try to maintain as much of a solution-focused stance as we can by introducing skills as something the clients can try and make their own judgment about, but we do take the lead in introducing them.

Debbie and John had real difficulty discussing their financial situation, which was dire. Discussions aimed at making financial plans typically erupted into shouted accusations by both partners and ended when John impulsively left the house. John was angry that Debbie made purchases for their two children that he considered frivolous, and Debbie complained that John maintained a weekly night out with his friends despite the cost involved. Both were discouraged by their situation and their struggles to work together to resolve it. In this case, we first used simple communication skill training to help Debbie and John stop making attributions about one another ("Debbie's just like her mother . . . all she does is spend and spend") and try to report their own worries more accurately ("I know you want to do nice things for the kids, but I'm scared we're going to lose our house and not have anywhere to live"). We also helped them slow down and listen more accurately to one another by teaching them reflective listening. As they were able to step out of the rounds of accusation and defense, they discovered that each felt very ashamed of their financial situation and that each blamed themselves as much as they blamed each other. With this discovery, they were able to begin looking together at options to improve their financial situation. By teaching some basic communication strategies, we were able to help Debbie and John decrease their conflict and return to a solution-focused approach to planning for the future and looking at times in the past when they had overcome adversity.

Other issues that sometimes arise include indications of psychological problems that need separate treatment, as in Frank's case; stressful life circumstances that can profit from case management or stress-reduction techniques; issues of grief or loss, again as in Frank's case; or substance abuse issues that are not being adequately treated. Our goal in each case is to resolve the constraint as quickly as we can to return to the focus on the couples, their successes, and their desired future. Figure 11.1 illustrates this process of evaluating and dealing with constraints.

ADAPTING THE MODEL TO A MULTICOUPLE GROUP FORMAT

Although the structure and general content of the treatment program are the same for both single-couple and multicouple groups, there are unique aspects of the multicouple group. We describe those in this section. The primary difference is the use of the session format to enhance the group process.

During their check-in after the presession meeting, the therapists first determine whether any couple is in such distress that they should not be included in the conjoint session. If there are no crises to be dealt with, the therapists briefly share the content of the check-in and try to identify common themes or issues that can be discussed in the conjoint group. For instance, if several couples report conflict about child issues, this could be a theme to be discussed. If several couples report struggling with angry interchanges, dealing with anger might be discussed. The themes serve to give most, if not all, couples a stake in what is being discussed rather than focusing on the specific problem of one couple while the rest listen.

The therapists begin the conjoint session by asking which couples would like to be "on the agenda" and start with the couple's content issues. As couples begin to discuss their content issues (e.g., a particular conflict they had over the weekend), the therapists use the themes identified during the therapist check-in to include other couples in the discussion. For instance, the therapist might turn to the group and say, "A number of you reported having a difficult time with conflict this weekend. What seemed to help you limit your fights?" Thus, other couples can be invited into the conversation and can share their own experiences specific to the general theme.

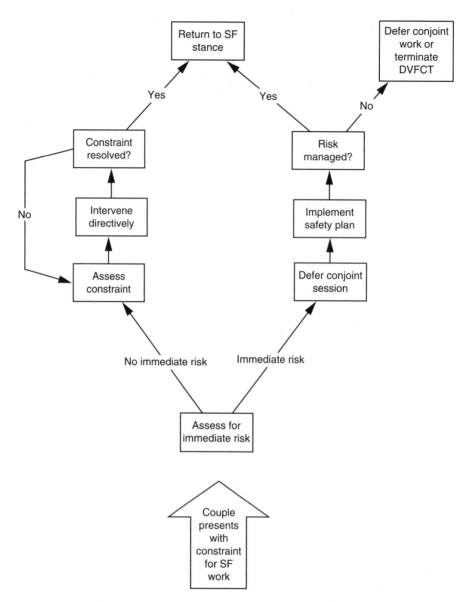

Figure 11.1. Process of evaluating and dealing with constraints to the solution-focused stance. DVFCT = domestic violence–focused couples therapy; SF = solution-focused.

As the focus of discussion shifts, the therapists continue to draw participants into the discussion by identifying and proposing common themes to the group. Over the course of the session, the therapists alternate between two roles. First, they may intervene directly with clients—asking direct questions, reframing, asking about exceptions, and so forth. This role looks more like the interaction a therapist would have with one couple during an individual session. We recommend that the therapists spend as little time as possible in this role. It may be needed when couple interaction becomes too intense and the therapist must intervene to lower it, when a couple raises an issue that the group is unwilling to address without the therapists' leadership, or when a couple is pushing away interaction with other group members.

In the second—and preferred—role, the therapist attends to the group process. In this case, the therapists do not intervene directly with individual couples. Instead, they work to maintain and use the group structure to achieve therapeutic goals. Components of this role include such things as the following:

- Making sure that group rules are being followed.
- Noticing when clients are quiet for long periods in the group and inviting them to participate. For example, "Marion, I notice you've been sitting quietly, but you look really thoughtful. I wonder how you see what we've been talking about."
- Linking the experiences of couples by drawing out commonalities and common themes. For example, "Seems like most of you had a good week by taking time to really talk to each other. What made that possible? What did each couple do to carve out some time to talk? I know you are all busy."
- Moderating the participation of couples so that no one couple monopolizes group time. Using common experiences to involve other couples is a face-saving way to shift the focus from a couple who are taking too much of the group's time. For example, Nguyen and Ahn had a particularly difficult style for the group to handle. They often raised the same issue and found it hard to move from complaining and accusing each other to looking for exceptions or solutions. The therapists intervened to focus on this process by saying, "It sounds like Ahn and Nguyen are stuck in a cycle that won't stop. All of you have been there. How did you break out of it? Tom, what did you do that helped you switch to looking for times that the problem didn't happen?"
- Pointing out group process issues when needed. For instance, the therapists might point out that the group seems stuck in a negative mind-set and it is difficult to look to the future with hope.

- Helping couples who are "out of phase" with where the majority of the members are in the group. For instance, if one couple has made significant progress while the rest of the group is still struggling, it may be difficult for the more successful couple to discuss their experiences of success. The therapists need to help the group understand that people move at different paces and there is room for all experiences.

While the preferred role for the therapists is that of working with the group process, therapists must be ready to shift roles when needed. Both roles are important and necessary for a successful group experience.

Many of our clients found the multicouple group a helpful experience. Particularly useful to a number of them was the interaction with other couples. One of our participants said this about the group:

It is that interaction with people, who have, for lack of a better word, I don't want to say suffered, but have had experience with similar circumstances . . . it provides comfort in knowing that you are not the only one, that other people have been through this and this is how they are willing to deal with it as the sessions proceed. But as well, some people heal faster than others so they are progressing at a faster rate, and the people in the group that are not progressing as quickly can learn from them.

Another participant also described the ways in which couples are able to learn from each other in the group format:

Client: Individual therapy would probably work after the group. But the nice thing about the group therapy, and the most common phrase I hear from all the women, and I hear it from the men is, "See! They do it!"

Interviewer: Now, what kind of "sees" are those about?

Client: When they say "see," they mean, basically, it's an observation from the spouse, saying to the other, "This is what they're experiencing. That same thing happens to us. Look how they deal with it. We should try that." There's no question, hearing suggestions and ideas from other couples is definitely helpful.

SOLIDIFYING CHANGE, TERMINATION, AND FOLLOW-UP

As the 12 weeks of Phase 2 draw to a close, the focus of treatment shifts to consolidating, punctuating, and planning for the maintenance of change. This is also a time for therapists and clients to assess progress and determine whether a referral for further treatment should be made. Several steps are involved in solidifying change.

Recognizing and Punctuating Change

As the conjoint phase comes to an end, it is important to help couples define and verbalize what changes they have made. It is likely that these changes will be the beginning of changing the couple relationship and not the end. Few couples end DVFCT in perfectly satisfying relationships. Some couples continue to amplify the changes they began to make during DVFCT, and others decide to continue couples therapy with another therapist. DVFCT often serves the purpose of helping couples become safe enough to participate in couples treatment approaches that are more expressive or experiential. Also as a part of ending treatment, we make clear the potential for relapse and help couples plan for it (as discussed later). However, this part of treatment is primarily a time to recognize the efforts that have been made and the steps taken toward changing the relationship and to make plans for expanding whatever positive steps have been made.

One way we help couples gauge and punctuate change is to help them formulate a vision of the "old couple" versus the "new couple." The old couple represents the state of their relationship when they entered treatment, and the new couple represents where they see themselves at present. We begin by asking the couple to try to envision the first day they came to DVFCT. What were they thinking? What were they feeling? What was going on in their relationship? We then ask them to reflect on the same questions as they would apply today. With these two reflections as representations of the old couple and the new couple, we then ask questions to draw out the differences. Useful questions might include the following: "What is the biggest difference between the old couple and the new couple?" "How would the old couple have dealt with the problems you've been facing recently?" "How did the new couple deal with them?" "What will be the signs in the future that the new couple is growing stronger and stronger?" "What positive parts of the old couple would you like to keep?"

Another facet of solidifying change is to project it into the future. Although we routinely use future-focused questions in DVFCT, we intentionally use questions to project into the future with the end of treatment near. Such questions can be formulated in any number of ways. One that we sometimes use at this stage is the crystal ball exercise. We ask the couple, "Suppose we had a crystal ball and we could look into the future. If the two of you keep going with the changes you've made, what will your relationship be like in 6 months? A year? What will each of you have contributed to getting it to that stage?"

Finally, some clients find it helpful to make a record of the changes they've made—a journal of change—and reread it from time to time. Ideally, this might be done at home and brought to the final session. The couple can share it with the therapists, who can comment on the changes recorded and add other changes that they have noticed.

Solidifying a Commitment to No Violence

The end of the conjoint phase of DVFCT is also a time when the couple's commitment to no violence can be solidified. We feel this is an important step to take no matter how well things have been going. Fundamentally, DVFCT is a treatment for partner aggression; helping couples see the changes they have made in this arena over the course of treatment and solidifying their commitment to no violence serves to keep this in focus until the end. We invite couples to decide what would be the most meaningful way for them to recommit to no violence. For some, this has involved creating and performing a ritual that makes concrete both partners' commitment to ending violence in their lives and their relationship. Others have made a certificate or picked an object (to display in their home) that is symbolic of their commitment.

Anticipating Challenges

Although a commitment to no violence is laudatory, and necessary, by itself it will likely not be enough to eliminate the potential for relapse. We also talk with couples about the potential for relapse and help them recognize the signs, specific to them, that may warn of impending relapse.

We have adopted the "emergency roadside repair kit" exercise (C. E. Johnson & Webster, 2002) as one planning tool for dealing with potential relapse. The metaphor of a roadside repair kit fits nicely because it suggests the common precautions we all take to deal with potential problems without putting potential relapse in the context of extraordinary vulnerability or dysfunction. Clients are asked first to recall what they keep in the trunk of their car to deal with unanticipated emergencies. As they enumerate the items, they can be asked if they are anticipating having a problem with their car anytime soon. Most clients reply that they are not; their emergency items are just normal precautions that people take in life. We remind the couple that they are on a journey themselves, a journey to a safe and satisfying relationship, and there are bound to be bumps in the road along the way. What items do they have in their "relationship roadside repair kit"? We then help them enumerate the resources they have that can help them when they encounter difficulty. We feel it is important to help them list both the intracouple resources they have (e.g., experience using time out successfully, having difficult conversations proactively rather than waiting until they blow up) as well as the extracouple resources they have (e.g., friends who are a support to them in difficult times, a return to therapy if need be).

Pichot and Dolan (2003) suggested several therapeutic benefits of the roadside repair kit metaphor. First, as noted earlier, it normalizes the potential for problems. It also helps to reinforce the fact that clients already have an array of resources at hand to cope with problems. Finally, Pichot and Dolan pointed out that the exercise empowers clients through preparation: By preparing, they are able to assume some control over life's inevitable ups and downs.

A second aspect of planning for challenges is to try to anticipate upcoming events that the couple will find stressful. Visits from family, holidays, and temporary layoffs can all be anticipated as occasions of heightened stress, and a plan can be formulated for handling them. One couple, for example, had a great deal of difficulty while visiting the wife's family. Planning for such an upcoming visit included deciding to stay in a hotel instead of with relatives, taking periodic "couple time-outs" from the family to relax and regroup, and having a secret signal the husband could use to let the wife know he needed some time alone.

In addition to planning for predictable events, it is also helpful for the couple to develop a "generic" stress management plan because many stressors are not easily anticipated. The loss of a job, sudden illness, and a child's school problems are all examples of things that might stress the couple but that cannot be predicted. Although called generic, the plan should be specific to the couple and can often be built on the vision of the new couple that the therapists help to develop at this stage. "How would the old couple deal with a problem that came up suddenly? How will the new couple deal with a problem like that?" As always, the more specific, concrete, and behavioral the plan, the more likely the couple will be able to recall it when need to.

Finally, there should be some discussion with the couple of signs that will reassure them that they are on track with the changes they are making and signs that they may need to come back to counseling.

Termination

The final session should be a celebration. We often end groups with an exercise in which we ask participants to talk individually about how they have changed and what ongoing work they see for themselves in the future. Then other participants summarize how they think the individual changed and what they see as the work left for him or her. Finally, the individual who spoke first gets to say something to the group. The following is an edited transcript of one such exercise. Luis is speaking to the group about his experience:

Luis: Something positive that I got out of the group . . . One thing is that it's possible to hear and mirror and validate somebody's feelings even if you don't agree with what they're saying. And something that I need to keep working on is, um, keeping perspective on when I— keeping perspective on my anger so that it remains local and proportional to what's happening. When it's not just to be avoided. I need to not see things as so big that I don't know what else to do but get out of here.

Therapist: All right. Now, we'll go around the room. A positive statement and something to work on for Luis.

Female Group Member: Oh, wow.

Therapist: What you see in Luis. Gains from the group. What he contributed, maybe, that you appreciate.

Female Group Member: Hmm. A lot of it is that he was learning to become more accountable and comfortable. And he could keep working on that . . . [Laughter].

Male Group Member: I think Luis's been very up forward with the way he feels about a lot of things. Up front. Not afraid to say how you feel, which isn't particularly a male characteristic, I don't think. So that's good. And I guess I agree with everyone else just to keep working on the trying to communicate and the stuff that we've learned here that you can keep doing it. That you keep doing it.

Male Group Member: I think you said something positive tonight. I think you were real pleased that you were able to mirror things, and you felt that you were able to look at things from your wife's perspective, you know, keep your calm, and I think you said that it was the first time in a couple of years that you had a good enough relationship to resolve things. And I think you've done really good about that, and I was glad to hear that. I think that was a real positive. I think you could keep on trying to work on those bases and realize that these fights probably aren't the end of the world, and it seems like there is a lot of threatening both ways of all or nothing—you do this and I'm gonna move out—I think those things are a lot of stress on both of you and that it's a kind of game or coping mechanism. So, for both of your sakes, you should try to realize that you're still here, and work on the positive and not to come up with your little threats because they are hurtful and after they become—they lose their meaning after a while, particularly when you come back the next day, and you do it every week, so it's a pattern. Just listen to each other and realize that hopefully those things aren't the end of the world and realize for the most part that you care about each other, and try to look at the positive and not just the negative and see what you've accomplished and you know, and realize that you're here because you care, and try to take what you've got as positive.

Therapist: OK, Luis, you get the last word on yourself, so if you want to comment, it's your floor.

Luis: Well, I appreciate all the positive things, and uh, the advice that you said. It's so meaningful to know that people were paying attention. So, thanks for being with me in this difficult time.

Alumni Group

One thing we learned early in our work in developing DVFCT is that 18 sessions is sometimes not enough to really solidify the changes couples have made. Many clients who have had positive experiences in the program were concerned that they could not remain in treatment longer than 18 sessions and felt some ongoing support would be useful. Therefore, we added an alumni group to our program. This group is led by cotherapists and generally meets twice a month. We maintain the structure of pre- and postsession meetings to monitor risk. The group operates within a solution-oriented framework, but the agenda is even more clearly in the hands of group members than it was during Phase 2. Group support and encouragement are strong aspects of the alumni group.

The group is open to couples who have completed either the multicouple group or individual couple treatment in DVFCT. We recommend getting five-session commitments from each couple and recommitting after five sessions. New group members can begin when each five-session module is complete. Beginning at the 5-week period allows for a stronger commitment and more continuity and support.

CONCLUSION

Although we continue to believe that couples counseling is not appropriate for all clients, the voices of our clients clearly express the need for domestic violence–focused couples counseling as an option for some. One female client told us:

> Well, if a couple has chosen to stay together, then they need some couples counseling sessions. I think it's essential. I don't think they'll ever be safe—they have hope to be safe if—I think we have some intense group members that have had very much more physical violence than I've ever known about in my life. They've brought up big issues in the group. And they've gone home and the next week they've had a great week.

12

OUR CLIENTS

In this chapter, we introduce some of our clients. Of course, the names and identifying information have been changed. We hope this chapter will give the reader some ideas about the diversity of the clients who have participated in our program. As you can see, some clients were able to end all forms of violence, some were able to reduce violence, and some chose (either unilaterally or bilaterally) to separate and end the relationship.

BOB AND MARY

Bob and Mary are an example of a couple who reduced their levels of violence. We recommended that they continue counseling after completing our program. Bob was a 45-year-old Caucasian with a bachelor's degree; he worked full time earning $20,000 to $39,000 a year. He learned about the program through an advertisement in the newspaper. Mary was a 48-year-old Caucasian with some college who was a full-time homemaker. They reported that they had been married for 11 years and were living together at time of treatment. They had four young children at home.

When they initially came to treatment, they said that there was not one specific incident that led them to seek help but a history of verbal abuse that often escalated to incidents of physical violence. Mary also reported that the children were clingy and she feared they would emulate the violence they saw in their parents' relationship. She hoped to prevent that by getting help. On the written pretest, they both reported that in the previous year they had shouted, yelled, insulted, and swore at one another and had thrown things; twisted the other's arm or hair; pushed or shoved; suffered a sprain, bruise, or cut; punched or hit the other; destroyed objects; slammed the other against a wall; and grabbed, slapped, and threatened to hit the other. Both also reported incidents of Mary choking Bob.

When they initially came to treatment, Mary reported that she wanted "to learn how to communicate again with her partner" and "to have respect for one another and learn how to deal with anger so that they can work better together as a couple with issues such as child rearing, finances, and intimacy." Bob reported that he "hopes for better understanding of one another, less violence, and better communication," to "learn how to control anger," and to "be able to work things out with one another."

Bob and Mary were randomly assigned to the multicouple group. At the end of treatment, Mary reported that they were "learning to be kind and be able to say they are sorry if they offend one another." Bob reported that he "recognizes better that verbal abuse is just as serious as physical abuse." However, both reported that during the 18 weeks of treatment, they both had shouted, yelled, insulted, and swore at the other. Mary also reported pushing and slapping Bob and that Bob had destroyed an object of hers and grabbed her.

When contacted 6 months after treatment, both reported being better able to negotiate, to call a time out when feelings were escalating, and that they were calmer and had better communication skills. They also hoped to continue their progress. However, on the follow-up survey, they both reported shouting, yelling, insulting, and swearing at their partner at least once since the end of treatment. Mary also reported that she pushed and grabbed Bob. Both reported that their partner had threatened to hit them.

It seemed to us that although the violence had decreased in frequency and severity, the couple needed ongoing treatment to eliminate it and to keep it from escalating again. We recommended further therapy for this couple.

MARIA AND JOSÉ

Maria and José are an example of a couple who decided to separate after completing treatment. They had been married 4 years before coming to treatment. They had two children, and she had a teenaged child from a previous relationship. She was a U.S. citizen and was sponsoring José for citizenship when they came to treatment. José was 35 and unemployed. He reported that he regularly used illegal drugs. They had both previously participated in couples counseling, and José had voluntarily attended a batterers program before the couple began our treatment program. Maria was 30 years old and worked part time in a variety of jobs.

When they came to the program, Maria reported that she wanted "better, calmer communication" and hoped "to gain greater understanding of her partner." She also said that she wanted a more secure relationship. José said that he "wanted better understanding and acceptance."

The incident that initially led them to seek therapy involved an argument in which José threw a soda in Maria's face. She responded by hitting and punching him, threatened to get a knife, and seized an umbrella to use as a weapon. He pulled her hair to get her off of him and then called the police. No arrest was made. In the pretest survey, they both reported using violence in the previous year. José reported throwing things, twisting her arm, pushing, shoving, punching, slamming against a wall, slapping, and threatening to hit. Maria reported throwing things, pushing, shoving, punching, slapping, grabbing, and kicking.

The couple was randomly assigned to individual treatment, and they completed treatment. While working individually with their counselors in the single-gender meetings and while working together, it became clear to both partners, and especially to Maria, that they could not stay together and still avoid violence. At the end of treatment, Maria reported that she had "gained more confidence in her perceptions of our situation and relationship." José reported that he "became less confident and less powerful in the relationship." On the posttest, they both reported ongoing violence during treatment. Jose reported throwing things, twisting her arm, and shoving, choking, slamming against wall, grabbing, and slapping her. Maria reported throwing, slamming him against a wall, and grabbing him.

At the end of treatment the couple separated, and Maria refused to sign papers to keep José from being deported. José did not expect to maintain any contact with his wife or their children after his deportation.

TOM AND ALICE

Tom and Alice—both 31—are an example of a couple who reduced their levels of violence and were recommended to continue treatment. Married 6 years, they were a Caucasian couple who both worked full time, and each made about $30,000 a year. They separated after the incident that brought them to therapy but moved back together when they started counseling. They had no children. At the pretest, Tom reported that he "wants help with his anger issues." Alice reported that she "wants couples treatment, so that they can maintain separate interests, grow together, and be happily married." They each reported being violent in their relationship, but Tom's violence was more frequent and of greater severity than Alice's. On the pretest inventory, both reported shouting, yelling, and swearing, as well as insulting, pushing, and kicking the other. Tom also threw things, twisted her arm or hair, punched or hit her, destroyed objects of hers, grabbed, slapped, and beat her up. The initial incident that led them to seek therapy was an argument with a lot of intimidation, screaming, and name-calling that escalated to Tom pushing Alice and punching her. He was arrested as a result of this incident and was court-ordered to batterer treatment before beginning the multicouple group. They completed treatment.

At the end of treatment, Alice reported a change in how she was responding to her husband. She also reported that "he is more patient and respectful"; "together we have matured and can discuss things better." She also indicated that she "wants these improvements to continue." Tom did not answer this question on the posttest. Neither partner reported perpetrating or receiving any physical violence at posttest. Both reported yelling, shouting, swearing, and insulting one another.

Six months after treatment, they completed the follow-up test. Tom reported that he was "willing to compromise more," that Alice was "less willing to hold a grudge," that "they resolve arguments faster and are less abusive." Alice reported that she was "better handling arguments and controlling my temper." She also indicated that she noticed more control in her partner and more of him putting forth an effort. She reported that she "feels they work better together and things are starting to feel normal." Both hoped their progress would continue in the future. However, both partners reported shouting, yelling, swearing, and insulting one another. Tom reported one incident in which he threw something at Alice and pushed her. We recommended continued to treatment for Tom and Alice.

SUSAN AND JOHN

Susan and John are an example of a couple who began treatment but dropped out when Susan decided to end the marriage. Both in their mid-40s, John and Susan are African American. They had no children. Both were employed full time, and their combined income was more than $100,000 a year. They had been married for 4 years before beginning treatment. John was court-ordered to batterer treatment. At intake, John stated that he "wanted to calm his anger and improve his communication." He also wanted the two of them "to be more understanding and peaceful at home" and hoped they could "both improve in their anger control and communication skills." Susan stated that she was "here because of her husband's wishes" and that she would like to learn to control her temper and had "no expectations for her husband or for their relationship." John reported that he threw things, broke things, punched walls, punched her, choked her, pushed her, pulled her hair, kicked her, restrained her, and grabbed her. Susan stated that she insulted and swore, pushed and shoved in self-defense, shouted and yelled, and kicked in self-defense.

The couple was assigned to single-couple treatment. It became evident during the initial interview that this case involved significant and serious issues. Susan confided to both therapists that the husband was portraying one set of relatively mild issues but that another, more serious set of issues were in place. John portrayed the incident that got him arrested as being an accident that was completely overblown. However, Susan maintained that her husband was verbally, emotionally, and physically abusive to her. She recounted instances when he demanded that she kneel in front of him so that he could slap her. The couple remained separate throughout treatment. During the process of the treatment, Susan enrolled in school and found an apartment near the campus. She did not let John know where she would be living. We helped Susan develop a safety plan and encouraged her to take his unpredictable behavior seriously. We also made sure that Susan could leave the sessions in plenty of time before John left each session. After the first session, we did not see the couple together. It became clear that Susan wanted to pursue a divorce from John. We discussed the potential for danger, and Susan stated that she was confident that she could handle the transition without any difficulty. We explained to John that there was no need for joint counseling at this time because they were divorcing and ended therapy after five sessions. Neither client returned to take the posttest, but Susan reported in a telephone call that the therapy helped her to make a decision to leave the relationship and that she had been able to leave safely.

BEN AND BARBARA

Ben and Barbara were able to end the violence in their relationship successfully. They were a Caucasian couple in their 50s who had been married 10 years. Ben earned more than $100,000 a year, and Barbara stayed home with their three children. They both had advanced degrees. They both wanted to stay together, but Barbara had made it clear that the marriage would end if there was one more violent incident. They both seemed to want to work toward a better and stronger relationship of mutual respect, and both said they wanted to "end all verbal, emotional, and physical abuse." Barbara answered the open-ended questions in the pretest in much greater detail and had clearly resolved (at least in writing) to leave Ben if any abuse continued.

Ben was arrested for punching Susan. He reported that he did not remember the incident in question, but he did know that it had happened. In his intake and initial phone contact, he said that he was shocked by his behavior and wanted to understand it. Ben said that he had not had a violent incident since he was 13 years old but that he wanted help with verbal abuse. Barbara reported in her intake that she had slapped her husband's face before.

The couple was randomly assigned to the multicouple group and completed treatment. At the end of treatment, both partners reported working on a positive relationship of mutual respect. Both reported that they had enjoyed being among a group of people with similar problems and talking them out. They both also reported positive changes in themselves and each other and a better level of communication. After completing treatment, they participated in the alumni group for over a year. At posttest and follow-up, neither partner reported any incidences of ongoing violence.

DAVID AND DONNA

David and Donna are also an example of a couple who was able to end the violence in their relationship. David was a 45-year-old Caucasian who made a salary of more than $50,000 a year. Donna, also Caucasian, was 40 years old and worked part time. They had been together 10 years and married 5 years when they came to treatment. They had three children.

Their initial goals for treatment were that they both wanted better communication and understanding. They both wanted the relationship to survive. David "did not want to dwell on the past, but focus on the future." Donna "wanted to focus on the good things and for them to be a team." The violence was unilateral male-to-female. When asked about what brought them to the program, Donna spoke about an incident when she was pregnant with their youngest child and David hit her in the back, hard, and she fell. They were self-referred and learned about our program through an advertisement in the newspaper. David reported on the pretest that he had pushed, shoved, punched, and destroyed an object of Donna's. Donna reported that she had grabbed David and had spat at him. David reported that the children "get upset when their parents argue." The couple participated in the multicouple group and completed treatment. At posttest, they reported that they "felt their children seemed more secure" and that their daughter "did not continually repeat how much she loved them." Neither partner reported any ongoing violence at posttest or 6 months after the 18-week treatment ended. They continued in the alumni group for about a year after completing treatment. They reported that their goal was to keep their improved relationship steady as they continued to feel more relaxed and caring toward one another. They are also noted that they were trying to take more time for the family. Donna noted that she felt that ongoing therapy would be necessary (at least once a month in the alumni group) to maintain the good patterns and to keep their anger in check. Donna reported that if they miss group, they "slip out of good practices."

Both Donna and David reported in the follow-up survey that they came close to meeting their goals and felt positive about their experience. Both noticed significant positive changes in themselves and their partner.

STEVEN AND SARAH

Steven and Sarah are also an example of a couple who was able to end the violence in their relationship. Steven was a 40-year-old U.S. citizen who was originally from South America. Sarah was a 43-year-old U.S. citizen who was originally from Turkey. They both worked full time, and each made about $30,000 a year. Steven was court-ordered to batterer intervention. They had been married for 7 years and had one child.

At the time of the pretest, Steven said his goal was "to improve himself, to be a better husband and father." He also wanted "them to be stronger as a couple." Sarah wanted "to work with her husband towards a better relationship so that the marriage will work." She hoped "they can live harmoniously, and respect one another in order to live a happy life." The violence was mostly unilateral male-to-female. On the pretest, Steven reported that he had insulted, shouted, and swore at Sarah; threw something; twisted her arm or hair; bruised or injured her; pushed, shoved, punched, hit, and grabbed her; slammed her against the wall; and slapped, threatened, and kicked Sarah during the past year. Sarah reported that she had shouted, insulted, swore at, and pushed Steven. The effect on their child was of grave concern for Sarah, who believed that their son was "around too much anger and it impacts his ability to concentrate, and contributes to his misbehaving in class." The couple reported that the child sometimes modeled his father's violent behavior. Steven and Sarah completed single-couple treatment.

At the end of treatment Steven reported "a dramatic improvement in physical violence" and that he was "being more understanding" and wanted "to continue to work on [the] relationship." Sarah stated that "as a couple [we] are more open and discuss" and "there is a more friendlier atmosphere at home." She felt "safe to express herself" and said that Steven "is nonviolent and will listen to her." Sarah reported that she "wants improvements to continue." Six months after completing treatment, Steven stated that "there is greater mutual respect," he was "aware of her feelings," and that Sarah "is more understanding." Sarah stated that "as a couple we have become closer and respect one another" and that Steven "is not violent." Both wanted to work toward maintaining changes that they had accomplished. By the end of treatment, they both reported that their son was much calmer and spending more time with father.

CONCLUSION

Not all clients participating in this program were able to end the violence and remain together. The goal of the program is to end all physical and psychological violence. When couples are able to end all forms of violence and remain together, we celebrate with them, but we also believe that couples who are able to separate nonviolently are successes. Acknowledging that it is not easy to change long-standing patterns of behavior, we recommend that clients who have successfully ended the violence continue participating in the alumni group or in another form of couples treatment at the end of the 18-week program.

13

OUR RESEARCH FINDINGS

As mentioned earlier in this book, domestic violence–focused couples therapy was originally developed as a part of a 3-year project funded by the National Institute of Mental Health. We randomly assigned clients to either multicouple group treatment or single-couple treatment. We collected quantitative data from clients before they began treatment, at the end of treatment, and 6 months after completing treatment. We collected qualitative data from surveys before we began treatment, at the end of every session, at the end of treatment, and 6 months after treatment. We also interviewed a subgroup of clients after the second, fifth, and final therapy sessions. We have continued to gather data since the end of the grant period. In this chapter, we present our research findings, using both quantitative and qualitative data.

RESULTS OF QUANTITATIVE RESEARCH

The sample we are using for data analysis varies by when it was collected. When we were originally funded, the focus of our work was to end male violence in relationships in which the couple chose to remain together.

Therefore, our primary research interest was in whether any male violence had occurred since beginning treatment. At the end of our funded study, 22 couples had completed the multicouple group program, and 20 couples had completed the single-couple treatment. Results from these groups were compared with those from a comparison group consisting of nine couples that had completed pretests and follow-up tests, but the couples were not able to participate in the couples intervention for a variety of reasons, primarily because of scheduling conflicts. Thirty percent of the couples assigned to the single-couple treatment, and 27% of the couples assigned to multicouple treatment dropped out before completing treatment. Six months after treatment, every female partner in each group was contacted. Those in the single-couple treatment condition reported a 43% recidivism rate, whereas those in the multicouple group treatment condition reported a 25% recidivism rate. Women in the comparison group reported a 67% recidivism rate (Stith, Rosen, McCullum, & Thomsen, 2004). Two years after treatment ended, 19 of the 30 wives completing treatment were contacted. Only two couples reported a subsequent violent incident (i.e., 13% recidivism). Four of the nine wives in the comparison group were contacted, and half reported a further violent episode by their partner, a 50% recidivism rate. We also asked about the couples' current marital status. Five of the 10 couples contacted from the single-couple condition and two of the 13 couples contacted from the multicouple group condition reported that they had divorced. Several wives who reported that they had divorced indicated that the couples counseling program gave them the courage to end the marriage. One wife reported that there had been no recurrence of violence because the counseling enabled her to get the courage she needed to state clearly that she would not tolerate any further violence. As soon as old patterns resurfaced that traditionally led to her partner being violent, she activated her safety plan before he could escalate. They are currently divorced. One wife reported that the couples counseling program made it possible for her to share custody with her husband after their divorce without ongoing violence. Another couple who successfully completed the multicouple group came in with low expectations. When contacted at 2-year follow-up, the wife said,

> I was very surprised that he was able to stop being violent—I had always heard that once a man is violent, he is always violent. So I am surprised and pleased that he could stop. Now he walks away when he feels himself becoming angry—he hasn't put a hand on me! We are really happy, and our relationship is so much better.

After completing the funded phase of the study, we continued collecting data. In the current analyses, 83 couples were randomly assigned to either multicouple or single-couple treatment. Of these, 55 couples completed the

TABLE 13.1
Domestic Violence–Focused Couples Therapy:
Significant Changes for Male and Female Participants

	Single couple (*n* = 17)	Multicouple group (*n* = 28)	Comparison (*n* = 9)
Physical aggression (partner report)	M, F	M, F	
Psychological aggression (partner report)	M	M, F	
Marital conflict		M, F	
Marital satisfaction	F	M, F	
Constructive communication	F	M, F	
Destructive communication		M	
Partner pursues, respondent distances	F	M	
Respondent pursues, partner distances		M	
Anger		M	
Anxiety		M	
Respondent differentiation	F	M, F	M
Partner differentiation		M, F	

Note. F = female participants; M = male participants.

program and the 6-month follow-up assessment. Nine couples served as the no-treatment comparison group. The analyses examined two broad domains. First, the impact of treatment on physical and psychological violence was examined using the Revised Conflict Tactics Scale (Straus, Hamby, Boney-McCoy, & Sugarman, 1996). In the second domain, a variety of both relational and individual issues were examined, including marital conflict (Level of Marital Conflict Scale; Straus, Gelles, & Steinmetz, 1980), anger (Novaco Anger Index; Novaco, 1976), anxiety (Symptom Checklist 90—Revised subscale; Derogatis, 1983), differentiation (Differentiation in Couple Relationship Scale; Anderson & Sabatelli, 1992), relationship satisfaction (Kansas Marital Satisfaction Scale; Schumm et al., 1983), communication, and pursue–distance patterns (Communication Patterns Questionnaire; Christensen & Sullaway, 1984).

Results of this research indicate that for both men and women, completing the 18-week program, either the single-couple or multicouple group, led to a significant reduction in physical violence toward their partner, as measured by partner reports. However, for men in particular, the multicouple group seemed to lead to a host of other benefits not seen in the single-couple condition (see Table 13.1). That is, partners of men in the multicouple group reported that the men were significantly less physically and psychologically abusive. Men who had participated in the multicouple group also reported that marital conflict decreased, relationship satisfaction increased, constructive communication increased, destructive communication decreased, and the use of the pursue–distance patterns decreased. Furthermore, men in the multicouple group reported decreased anger, decreased anxiety, increased differentiation, and increased partner differentiation. The only significant changes noted for males in the single-couple condition were that their partners reported that they were less physically and psychologically abusive. Therefore, it seems to us that the multicouple group condition leads to more benefits for men (and therefore for the partners of abusive men).

For women, the pattern is less clear, with a mix of benefits spread between the two formats (see Table 13.1). Partners of women in both the multicouple and single-couple conditions reported that they were less physically abusive after completing treatment. Also, women in both modalities reported increases in marital satisfaction, constructive communication, and respondent differentiation. However, only women in the multicouple group were reported by their partners to be less psychologically abusive, and only these women reported significant reductions in marital conflict and partner differentiation. In contrast, only women in the single-couple condition reported reduction in partner pursues–respondent distances. Furthermore, women in our project did not report reductions in destructive communication, respondent pursues–partner distances, anger, or anxiety. Because the primary purpose of the 18-week program is to reduce or eliminate violence, we are pleased that both modalities were effective in reducing physical aggression for both male and female participants, but we are continuing to develop and test both methods of delivering the treatment model to improve the ability of both modalities to treat both men and women.

QUALITATIVE CHANGES

In addition to wanting to know from standardized research measures whether our clients made changes, we also wanted to hear from them about their experiences in our treatment program. We gave them many opportunities to share their thoughts with us. Some of these quotes have been inserted throughout the book. Here we summarize other feedback we received from clients.

Short-Answer Responses to the Follow-Up Survey

We asked all clients to complete an end-of-treatment survey on the changes they or their partner made during the program. We learned from women or their partners that women made changes in five categories: empowerment, lower reactivity, increased hopefulness, increased patience toward partner, and more involvement in the relationship. Some quotes from these surveys made by women included the following: "Free to be myself. I look for the positive in my spouse. I'm more direct in expressing my needs"; "feel more secure in our relationship"; "have more hope that we can work out our difficulties without resorting to verbal, emotional, or physical abuse"; and "increase in self-identity and individual goals." Some quotes from partners of these women when asked about changes they noted in their female partners included "more involved"; "greater acceptance of different opinions and anger coping mechanisms"; "understanding me a little more; catching herself when she is getting really frustrated."

Men or their partners reported that the males changed in seven areas: improved stress and anger management skills, more trust, broader perspective, more consideration, greater ability and desire to communicate, and more accepting of partner. Quotes from men in response to a question about changes they made include "not letting stress build up; not throwing objects, and staying pretty calm"; "I am more considerate of my wife's feelings and points of view"; "I do not speak for [wife]"; "less jealousy"; and "think more how my actions (speech) affect her." Women also reported changes in their male partners, for example: "less likely to [resort to] violent behavior"; "talking more, compromising"; "My spouse is more sensitive, supportive, and more there for me emotionally. He is making great efforts to lessen stress in my life"; "no hitting; no bad language."

In addition to asking clients about changes they noted in their own and their partner's behavior, we asked in many ways (i.e., end-of-session feedback forms, end-of-treatment surveys, in-person interviews) about what they did and did not like about particular sessions or about treatment in general. We have used this feedback to improve the program. First, we report summaries of what clients said that they did not like and how we addressed these concerns. Next, we report on client responses concerning what they did like from the various mechanisms we used to get their feedback.

What Clients Did Not Like

Of course, clients reported concerns on their weekly feedback sheets, in their end-of-therapy written evaluations, and in their in-person interviews. As mentioned earlier, some of these concerns changed over time. For example, early on, some clients were concerned about the focus on positives and wanted us to get into more depth with problems. As a result of this feedback, we designed the first session to "honor the problem." We also found many clients reported over time that they began to see value in the focus on positives.

Some clients were frustrated that the program lasted for only 18 weeks. They thought they were "opening up a can of worms" and 18 weeks was not sufficient time to make such major changes. As a result of this feedback, we added an alumni group. Clients have the option to sign up for an ongoing alumni group for as long as they choose, but the core treatment program remains 18 weeks in duration. We find that it is helpful for clients to know how long treatment lasts. Some clients also expressed concern about the amount of time we spent on safety planning, time outs, and recognizing escalation signals because they did not think they really had a problem with violence. However, we continue to believe that if there has been violence in the past, it can recur, and we want to be as careful as possible that conjoint treatment does not increase its likelihood. At this point, we have never had a client report that anything that happened in the session led to a recurrence of violence.

Some clients, especially men, also expressed concerns about the pre–post session check-ins. In general, pre- and post-meetings tend to last longer with female clients and to be shorter with male clients. Although many clients, particularly the women, mentioned that they really liked the check-ins, some did not find them useful. In fact, one man in the multicouple group thought they were destructive:

> I think it's harmful . . . destructive. It's time that could be spent in the . . .
> I think the most beneficial part of the group is when there's like a round
> robin, and the couples are talking about different methods they've used
> to help organize their lives.

Although most clients over time began to see the value of check-ins, it is also possible that this program might not be suitable for everyone. We also had clients who had concerns about the young age of some of the cotherapists, about a therapist not holding their partner accountable in a particular session, or about whether difficult, painful issues might have been ignored to keep things on a positive note. We sometimes heard about difficult issues in the presession check-ins, and the person experiencing the problems did not want to address the issue with her partner. We respect clients' decisions on this, but some clients have expressed concerns that we did not challenge the partner. We continue to work on balancing safety, looking at strengths while not ignoring painful issues.

What Was Helpful in the End-of-Session Evaluation Forms

As discussed in Chapter 10, we ask clients to complete evaluation forms after each session, and we use these responses to guide upcoming sessions. Here we organize the responses to this survey by single-couple and multicouple group. Far and away, the most common response to the question of what was helpful in single-couple counseling fell into a category we called "couple communication." Clients wrote about how talking with each other in the session was helpful. A woman wrote, for example, "I was able to share something that I'd never shared before that was a really big problem." Participants also mentioned finding it useful when their partner heard something they had expressed. A man wrote, "I felt like I was listened to and heard." A final component of couple communication was being able to discuss contentious issues safely while in session. A woman wrote that the most helpful thing about one session was the experience of "being able to express a heated issue in a safe environment." Clients in the single-couple condition also frequently described aspects of the therapeutic relationship that were helpful. Clients wrote about therapists helping them feel safe. Finally, consonant with the solution-focused model that forms the basis of this treatment, participants mentioned the usefulness of the therapists pointing out strengths and competencies in both partners in addition to discussing problems. For example, a female client wrote that the most helpful part of the entire process for her was "positive highlighting in each session no matter how negative we were about each other." Clients in both conditions mentioned many times that working together as a couple to learn the time-out procedure and other anger management skills had been helpful to them. Clients in the single-couple condition also mentioned learning new ideas and perspectives.

When asked what had been helpful in the multicouple group session, clients most frequently mentioned group process factors. Many participants mentioned the importance of locating their experiences in a social context. They said that it was helpful simply to hear the stories of other people who struggled with the same issue of violence in marriage. A male participant said that the most helpful thing for him was "hearing experiences of other couples, how they tried approaches, their feelings and reactions." Participants also said that a feeling of caring developed between group members over time and that this was useful. It is probably not surprising that couples found the opportunity to talk with others in the same situation helpful. We can conjecture that marital violence is not a typical topic of social conversation and that the opportunity to discuss it openly breaks some of the sense of isolation that may come from living with such a secret. In fact, breaking social isolation is one of the factors cited by Yalom (1995) as a curative factor in group psychotherapy in general. Group members felt that they learned from each other. For example, a man remarked that he had found one session helpful because "all couples [were] very open and helpful in giving advice and views." Finally, several participants mentioned that it had been useful to them to see other couples make progress in strengthening their relationships. A male participant said one session was helpful because he "heard how other couples were successfully progressing communicating."

Participants in the multicouple group also reported that they found the chance to communicate as a couple helpful. They also reported learning more about how to communicate from the therapists' guidance, the example of others, and their own practice. They reported, as did the couples in the single-couple condition, that learning anger management skills was helpful. Many clients in the multicouple group also reported that learning time-out procedures was helpful.

QUALITATIVE IN-PERSON INTERVIEWS

Seventeen couples were interviewed from one to four times during their treatment experience. Most were interviewed at the beginning, middle, and end of treatment. Seventy-five 30-minute interviews were analyzed, including two telephone interviews with couples who dropped out of treatment and two focus group interviews with couples participating in our alumni group.

Most participants reported that they believed therapy was helpful overall regardless of whether the therapeutic outcome was what they had hoped it would be (e.g., improving the relationship vs. ending the relationship). Some participants expressed specific areas of dissatisfaction. Many of the complaints were voiced by clients who were in the early stages of treatment but were no longer an issue by the time treatment ended. As discussed earlier, many of the complaints that were voiced early in the project have resulted in changes in the protocol.

Therapeutic Relationship

As in the short-answer responses, when asked what they found helpful in the interviews, the most frequent response was in the area of the alliance or client–therapist relationship. Clients used words or phrases such as "caring," "listening," "understanding what is being said," "respectful," "competent," and "nonjudgmental" to describe their therapists. Developing a strong therapeutic alliance seemed to make clients feel safe and comfortable. For example, when asked about what came to mind for her when she thought about her last session, one woman responded first with, "Well, I just feel so safe, number one. So comfortable." Another woman told the interviewer that normally she was hesitant to share her feelings with anyone, but because she felt comfortable with her therapists, she found herself talking a lot.

Establishing a positive therapeutic relationship may be doubly important for couples involved in treatment for domestic violence because of the shame that often accompanies this problem and the feeling of being blamed on both the man's and the woman's part. One man expressed this sense of vulnerability when he was asked what came to mind when he thought about his first two sessions:

When I think of those sessions, what comes to mind is that we're going to open up our lives and share our lives with some folks who are supposed to be there to help us in some way, and so far I've been pretty much pleased with the sessions. [The therapists] are very good at . . . sharing with us and asking the right questions to get the proper understanding.

It appears that this client was already developing a sense of trust that the therapists were competent and had his interests in mind.

Feeling accepted and valued also seemed to reduce the potential for resistance. One woman contrasted the treatment she experienced in this program with other marital therapy experiences in terms of feeling blamed in earlier treatment and in which her reaction was to "push it away" or not accept what the counselor was saying. In contrast, she reported feeling comfortable and safe in this program and finding what the therapists said meaningful to her:

I mean I just feel so comfortable and so safe and just the things they pick up on are so meaningful and I just have a very . . . this is a very positive experience, more probably than I would have hoped for, because my experience in the past with joint [therapy] with [husband] have been such a nightmare for me. . . . In the past, there's been so many counseling sessions, where I'd just . . . I would push it away, as far . . . when I was being told I was controlling my husband . . . I'm sorry I mean, I just pushed that as far away. . . . She [previous therapist] was blaming me, blaming, me, and my husband was blaming me. I think part of that is that neither of the counselors here put us on the defensive, or let the situation go to the point where we feel like we have to defend ourselves. I think that's been very different than what I've experienced in the past.

Other critical components of a strong therapeutic alliance reported by our clients included listening, understanding the client's meaning, and being respectful and tuned in to clients. Clients are also better able to trust therapists who are genuine and who seem like real people. Most of our clients felt that our therapists demonstrated those qualities.

Therapeutic Interventions

In addition to discussing aspects of the therapeutic alliance, clients spoke about therapeutic interventions. A number of clients highlighted the value of the program's focus on strengths. For example, a female client and a male client discussed the focus on strengths.

Female Client: No judgments! In fact, every time you go in, they pick up on positive things on both of us. They make it a point to bring out what they see that's good, and I just see that as very professional and just not what I've had in the past. . . . I think they are making that balance again.

> They're giving both of us positive feedback. . . . When I leave here at night I would expect in the past for him to have been withdrawn from me and distant. It's just the opposite.

Male Client: [The therapist] asks us to think of the times when my wife and I are kind to each other, to make notes of it. To focus on that kind of relationship. Also to make notes of the times that we are kind to each other. I think that is helpful.

Clients also spoke positively about being given homework because they liked to have work to do between sessions. Many spoke about the helpfulness of learning the time-out procedure. Clients also spoke about the process our cotherapists use to communicate with each other during the session (i.e., meta-dialogue). This type of "public talk" is a method of inquiry because it not only allows clients to "see inside" their therapist, it also stimulates them to think differently about their own situation. Although clients did not know what this intervention is called, several commented on its usefulness.

Female Client: It was extremely helpful when the two counselors would compare notes on what they heard from each of us. Reflecting on what was heard created a sense of us viewing our relationship from the outside looking in. It was a different way of seeing or hearing how we are reading one another. This was extremely helpful.

Male Client: I like the way [the therapists] consult with each other on how they're perceiving what we're saying, and so forth.

Several clients seemed to feel that it was helpful to have therapists there to witness, confirm, and validate what they were experiencing. One woman said, "I have someone there, even if he [husband] does not understand what I am saying, someone in the room understands what I'm saying. I'm not crazy. OK. So that's good."

Therapy Structure

When clients were asked what was helpful, some gave an answer that related to how the therapy was structured. These responses were placed into one of two categories: pre–post session check-ins or cotherapists. Several clients mentioned that they liked having individual (or separate-gender) time with their therapist before or after the session (or both). For some, this process seemed to provide an opportunity to vent without doing so in front of their partner; for others, it was an opportunity to direct the focus of the conjoint portion of the session. In addition, if there had been violence in the preceding week, being able to talk about it was important for some clients.

> Male Client: It seems that [the session] is focused and tailored to at least what I've talked about in the presession. To be able to do that on the fly is pretty good.

> Male Client: What is nice too about the way they conduct the sessions is that when they do get us apart, both of us are able to speak more liberally. Because, I know [wife] is sensitive in some areas, so there are times when I have to choose my words carefully and what I want to say to express what I really mean . . . and in choosing the words carefully, sometimes I don't really get out what I really mean.

> Female Client: It's helpful because it is supportive for the girls. When we go into the class with the guys and girls and I have had a hard week with my husband and we've yelled and he's thrown things around the house and he's done all this stuff, I really can't talk to anybody because I'm afraid that he is going to do something. So by going in and talking to the women first it kind of gets it off my chest and they know about it, they'll bring it up.

Clients also spoke about the value of having cotherapists, and especially male–female cotherapists. For example, one female client spoke about how much she liked having two therapists.

> Female Client: It's just so plain and simple and natural that men and women are different and they were both open and gave a lot of insight. It was open about the differences and giving a man's point of view and pointing things out like that. Instead of someone saying, "Well, I think that this is how men are," if it was a woman. If it was just a man I think that would be even more difficult. . . . Two different people can do that.

> Male Client: One of the main things that I find to be helpful . . . we've gone to several counselors before. Some I felt a bias between whether we got a female or a male, and I really like the fact that we have a man and a woman, together, and that's where I feel that both of us can be very much understood. . . . And I feel that they can come together and discuss the male and female perspective of it and help us to get a better understanding of that, maybe.

Clients in the face-to-face interviews also spoke about learning communication skills, time out, having time to talk, and being able to express their feelings. Clients also spoke about the value of the conjoint session in enhancing accountability.

Female Client: Well, he was accountable to two rational human beings, you know, so he couldn't just laugh it off, and just make it like nothing occurred or he hadn't done anything. I think that was crucial and they, they were asking questions.

Male Client: 'Cause we think about it and we think, "Well, we are going back next Tuesday night and if we act like complete butts, we are going to have to go in there and talk about it," so you know, that is one thing to keep you in check. People keep other people in check, you know, a lot. Which is a good thing.

Participants also spoke in the face-to-face interviews about how helpful various group process factors were, such as making them feel less isolated, peer support, vicarious communication, gaining perspective, and peer confrontation. Women, in particular, noted the value of group confrontation.

Female Client: They will gang up on each other [the men]. Which works for a little while, even after the session. The guys will gang up on one particular person and say, "You were really rude to your wife, and you really shouldn't be doing that." It seems to calm them down.

Female Client: Then we get back together and you can tell when the other partner is lying, like if another couple is lying, I will say, "Are you sure you didn't throw the chair at her?" and he'll say, "Oh, maybe I did."

Clients also spoke about learning from each other in the multicouple group. Sometimes they mentioned active learning when group members gave each other advice or suggested things they could try. Other types of learning were more indirect, such as learning by watching other couples work out their problems. At other times, they noted that they had learned something from seeing their own struggles in other couples' relationships. One male client said,

They [another couple] came up with an excellent idea for the marriage management meeting. If I hadn't been in the group, I wouldn't have ever thought of it, at least not for a while. There's no question, hearing suggestions and ideas from other couples is definitely helpful.

FUTURE RESEARCH

Research on this treatment program is ongoing. We are continuing to develop the program and to make it more effective for aggressive women. The treatment program is being compared with a different program in a randomized control trial funded by the National Science Foundation. We have adapted the program, and it has been used in Mexico; we are also interested in testing the effectiveness of the program with different cultural groups and with same-sex couples. Many of the groups that are using the program are considering it an early intervention or prevention program to prevent the escalation of psychological and low levels of violence.

CLOSING

Intimate partner violence remains a difficult and costly social problem that severely disrupts the lives of the families. Despite decades of dedicated work by law enforcement personnel, the court system, victim advocates, batterer intervention program providers, therapists, and researchers, definitive solutions to this problem remain elusive. We hope that our work with couples like the ones described in Chapter 12 can become part of what we are convinced must be a communitywide effort to help families and couples. We have consistently been touched by the suffering of our clients and often awestruck at the efforts they have made to lessen that suffering and find happier, more peaceful lives. Although we believe that our approach to couples treatment for intimate partner violence attends to both safety and change, we are also aware that much work remains to be done. We hope that our efforts will be a stepping stone in the process of finding better ways to help families flourish in an atmosphere free of violence.

SUGGESTED READINGS

Domestic Violence

Campbell, J. (Ed.). (2007). *Assessing dangerousness: Violence by batterers and child abusers* (2nd ed.). New York, NY: Springer.

Cooper, J., & Vetere, A. (2005). *Domestic violence and family safety: A systemic approach to working with violence in families.* London, England: Whurr.

Hamel, J., & Nicholls, T. (Eds.). (2007). *Family interventions in domestic violence: A handbook of gender-inclusive theory and treatment.* New York, NY: Springer.

Harway, M., & O'Neil, J. M. (Eds.). (1999). *What causes men's violence against women?* Thousand Oaks, CA: Sage.

Jacobson, N. S., & Gottman, J. M. (1998). *When men batter women: New insights into ending abusive relationships.* New York, NY: Simon & Schuster.

Jenkins, A. (1990). *Invitations to responsibility: The therapeutic engagement of men who are violent and abusive.* Adelaide, Australia: Dulwich Center.

Johnson, M. P. (2008). *A typology of domestic violence: Intimate terrorism, violent resistance, and situational couple violence.* Lebanon, NH: Northeastern University Press.

Jordan, C. E., Nietzel, M. T., Walker, R., & Logan, T. K. (2004). *Intimate partner violence: A clinical training guide for mental health professionals.* New York, NY: Springer.

Malley-Morrison, K., & Hines, D. A. (2004). *Family violence in a cultural perspective: Defining, understanding, and combating abuse.* Thousand Oaks, CA: Sage.

Mills, L. G. (2003). *Insult to injury: Rethinking our responses to intimate abuse.* Princeton, NJ: Princeton University Press.

Mills, L. G. (2008). *Violent partners: A breakthrough plan for ending the cycle of abuse.* Philadelphia, PA: Basic Books.

O'Leary, K. D., & Woodin, E. M. (Eds.). (2009). *Psychological and physical aggression in couples: Causes and interventions.* Washington, DC: American Psychological Association.

Walker, L. E. (2000). *The battered woman syndrome* (2nd ed.). New York, NY: Springer.

Whitaker, D. J., & Lutzker, J. R. (Eds.). (2009). *Preventing partner violence: Research and evidence-based intervention strategies.* Washington, DC: American Psychological Association.

Meditation

Carrington, P. (1998). *The book of meditation: The complete guide to modern meditation.* Boston, MA: Element.

Gunaratana, B. G. (1996). *Mindfulness in plain English* (2nd ed.). Somerville, MA: Wisdom.

Kabat-Zinn, J. (1994). *Wherever you go, there you are: Mindfulness meditation in everyday life*. New York, NY: Hyperion.

Solution-Focused Brief Therapy

de Shazer, S. Dolan, Y., Korman, H., Trepper, T., McCollum, E., & Berg, I. K. (2007). *More than miracles: The state of the art of solution-focused brief therapy*. New York, NY: Haworth Press.

Lipchik, E., & Kubicki, A. (1996). Solution-focused domestic violence views: Bridges toward a new reality in couples therapy. In S. D. Miller, M. A. Hubble, & B. L. Duncan (Eds.), *Handbook of solution-focused brief therapy* (pp. 65–97). San Francisco, CA: Jossey-Bass.

McCollum, E. E., & Trepper, T. S. (2001). *Family solutions for substance abuse: Clinical and counseling approaches*. New York, NY: Haworth Press.

Pichot, T., & Dolan, Y. (2003). Solution-focused brief therapy: Its effective use in agency settings. New York, NY: Haworth Press.

REFERENCES

Aldarondo, E., & Straus, M. A. (1994). Screening for physical violence in couple therapy: Methodological, practical, and ethical considerations. *Family Process, 33*, 425–439. doi:10.1111/j.1545-5300.1994.00425.x

Anderson, S. A., & Sabatelli, R. M. (1992). The Differentiation in the Family System Scale (DIFS). *American Journal of Family Therapy, 20*, 77–89.

Archer, J. (2002). Sex differences in physically aggressive acts between heterosexual couples: A meta-analytic review. *Aggression and Violent Behavior, 7*, 313–351. doi:10.1016/S1359-1789(01)00061-1

Babcock, J. C., Green, C. E., & Robie, C. (2004). Does batterers' treatment work? A meta-analytic review of domestic violence treatment. *Clinical Psychology Review, 23*, 1023–1053. doi:10.1016/j.cpr.2002.07.001

Babor, T. F., Higgins-Biddle, J. C., Saunders, J. B., & Monteiro, M. G. (2001). *AUDIT: The Alcohol Use Disorders Test: Guidelines for use in primary care.* Geneva, Switzerland: World Health Organization.

Baer, R. A. (2003). Mindfulness training as a clinical intervention: A conceptual and empirical review. *Clinical Psychology: Science and Practice, 10*, 125–143. doi:10.1093/clipsy/bpg015

Bowen, S., Witkiewitz, K., Dillworth, T. M., Chawla, N., Simpson, T. L., Ostafin, B. D., . . . Marlatt, G. A. (2006). Mindfulness meditation and substance use in an incarcerated population. *Psychology of Addictive Behaviors, 20*, 343–347. doi:10.1037/0893-164X.20.3.343

Brannen, S. J., & Rubin, A. (1996). Comparing the effectiveness of gender-specific and couples groups in a court-mandated spouse abuse treatment program. *Research on Social Work Practice, 6*, 405–424. doi:10.1177/104973159600600401

Brehm, S. S., & Brehm, J. W. (1981). *Psychological reactance: A theory of freedom and control.* New York, NY: Academic Press.

Breunlin, D. C., Schwartz, R. C., & MacKune-Karrer, B. (1992). *Metaframeworks: Transcending the models of family therapy.* San Francisco, CA: Jossey-Bass.

Burns, D. B. (1999). *Feeling good: The new mood therapy. The clinically proven drug-free treatment for depression.* New York, NY: HarperCollins.

Carrington, P. (1998). *The book of meditation: The complete guide to modern meditation.* Boston, MA: Element.

Chermack, S. T., & Blow, F. C. (2002). Violence among individuals in substance abuse treatment: The role of alcohol and cocaine consumption. *Drug and Alcohol Dependence, 66*, 29–37. doi:10.1016/S0376-8716(01)00180-6

Chermack, S. T., Fuller, B. E., & Blow, F. C. (2000). Predictors of expressed partner and non-partner violence among patients in substance abuse treatment. *Drug and Alcohol Dependence, 58*, 43–54. doi:10.1016/S0376-8716(99)00067-8

185

Christensen, A., & Sullaway, M. (1984). *Communication Patterns Questionnaire*. Unpublished manuscript, University of California, Los Angeles.

Coker, A. L., Davis, I., Arias, I., Desai, S., Sanderson, M., Brandt, H., & Smith, P. (2002). Physical and mental health effects of intimate partner violence for men and women. *American Journal of Preventive Medicine, 23*, 260–268. doi:10.1016/S0749-3797(02)00514-7

de Shazer, S., Dolan, Y., Korman, H., Trepper, T., McCollum, E., & Berg, I. K. (2007). *More than miracles: The state of the art of solution-focused brief therapy*. Binghamton, NY: Haworth Press.

Derogatis, L. R. (1983). SCL-90-R: Administration, scoring, and procedures manual— II (2nd ed.). Towson, MD: Clinical Psychometric Research.

Derogatis, L. R., & Melisaratos, N. (1983). The Brief Symptom Inventory: An introductory report. *Psychological Medicine, 13*, 595–605. doi:10.1017/S0033291700048017

Dunford, F. W. (2000). The San Diego Navy experiment: An assessment of interventions for men who assault their wives. *Journal of Consulting and Clinical Psychology, 68*, 468–476. doi:10.1037/0022-006X.68.3.468

Edleson, J. L., & Tolman, R. M. (1992). *Intervention for men who batter: An ecological approach*. Newbury Park, CA: Sage.

Fals-Stewart, W., Kashdan, T. B., O'Farrell, T. J., & Bircher, G. R. (2002). Behavioral couples therapy for drug abusing patients: Effects on partner violence. *Journal of Substance Abuse Treatment, 22*, 87–96. doi:10.1016/S0740-5472(01)00218-5

Feld, S. L., & Straus, M. A. (1989). Escalation and desistence of wife assault in marriage. *Criminology, 27*, 141–162. doi:10.1111/j.1745-9125.1989.tb00866.x

Foran, H. M., & O'Leary, K. D. (2008). Alcohol and intimate partner violence: A meta-analytic review. *Clinical Psychology Review, 28*, 1222–1234. doi:10.1016/j.cpr.2008.05.001

Fruzzetti, A. E., & Levensky, E. R. (2000). Dialectical behavior therapy for domestic violence: Rationale and procedures. *Cognitive and Behavioral Practice, 7*, 435–447. doi:10.1016/S1077-7229(00)80055-3

Gelles, R. J., & Straus, M. A. (1988). *Intimate violence*. New York, NY: Simon & Schuster.

Gondolf, E. W. (1988). Who are those guys? Toward a behavioral typology of batterers. *Violence and Victims, 3*, 187–203.

Gondolf, E. W. (1998). The victims of court-ordered batterers: Their victimization, helpseeking, and perceptions. *Violence Against Women, 4*, 659–676. doi:10.1177/1077801298004006003

Gottman, J. (1999). *The marriage clinic: A scientifically based marital therapy*. New York, NY: Norton.

Graham-Kevan, N., & Archer, J. (2005). Investigating three explanations of women's relationship aggression. *Psychology of Women Quarterly, 29*, 270–277.251658240 doi:10.1111/j.1471-6402.2005.00221.x

Grossman, P., Niemann, L., Schmidt, S., & Walach, H. (2004). Mindfulness-based stress reduction and health benefits: A meta-analysis. *Journal of Psychosomatic Research, 57,* 35–43. doi:10.1016/S0022-3999(03)00573-7

Haley, J. (1976). *Problem-solving therapy: New strategies for effective family therapy.* San Francisco, CA: Jossey-Bass.

Hansen, M., Harway, M., & Cervantes, N. (1991). Therapists' perceptions of severity in cases of family violence. *Violence and Victims, 6,* 225–235.

Hanson, R. (2009). *Buddha's brain: The practical neuroscience of happiness, love and wisdom.* Oakland, CA: New Harbinger.

Hart, B. (1988). *Safety for women: Monitoring batterers' programs* [manual]. Harrisburg: Pennsylvania Coalition Against Domestic Violence.

Henderson, A., Bartholomew, K., Trinke, S., & Kwong, M. (2005). When loving means hurting: An exploration of attachment and intimate abuse in a community sample. *Journal of Family Violence, 20,* 219–230. doi:10.1007/s10896-005-5985-y

Holtzworth-Munroe, A., Beatty, S. B., & Anglin, K. (1995). The assessment and treatment of marital violence: An introduction for the marital therapist. In N. S. Jacobson & A. S. Gurman (Eds.), *Clinical handbook of couple therapy* (pp. 317–339). New York, NY: Guilford Press.

Holtzworth-Munroe, A., & Stuart, G. L. (1994). Typologies of male batterers: Three subtypes and the differences among them. *Psychological Bulletin, 116,* 476–497. doi:10.1037/0033-2909.116.3.476

Ingersoll, K. S., Wagner, C. C., & Gharib, S. (2002). *Motivational groups for community substance abuse programs* (2nd ed.). Richmond, VA: Mid-Atlantic Addiction Technology Transfer Center.

Johnson, C. E., & Webster, D. (2002). *Recrafting a life.* New York, NY: Taylor and Francis.

Johnson, M. P. (1995). Patriarchal terrorism and common couple violence: Two forms of violence against women. *Journal of Marriage and the Family, 57,* 283–294. doi:10.2307/353683

Johnson, M. P. (2000, November). *Conflict and control: Symmetry and asymmetry in domestic violence.* Paper presented at the National Institute of Justice Gender Symmetry Workshop, Arlington, VA.

Johnson, M. P. (2006). Conflict and control: Gender symmetry and asymmetry in domestic violence. *Violence Against Women, 12,* 1003–1018. doi:10.1177/1077801206293328

Johnson, M. P., & Ferraro, K. J. (2000). Research on domestic violence in the 1990s: Making distinctions. *Journal of Marriage and the Family, 62,* 948–963. doi:10.1111/j.1741-3737.2000.00948.x

Jordan, C. E., Nietzel, M. T., Walker, R., & Logan, T. K. (2004). Intimate partner violence: A clinical training guide for mental health professionals. New York, NY: Springer.

Jose, A., & O'Leary, K. D. (2009) Prevalence of partner aggression in representative and clinic samples. In K. D. O'Leary & E. M. Woodin (Eds.), *Psychological and physical aggression in couples: Causes and interventions*. Washington, DC: American Psychological Association.

Kabat-Zinn, J. (1990). *Full catastrophe living: Using the wisdom of your body and mind to face stress, pain and illness*. New York, NY: Delacorte.

Kantor, G. K., & Straus, M. A. (1989). Substance abuse as a precipitant of wife abuse victimizations. *The American Journal of Drug and Alcohol Abuse, 15*, 173–189. doi:10.3109/00952998909092719

Maiuro, R. D., & Eberle, J. A. (2008). State standards for domestic violence perpetrator treatment: Current status, trends, and recommendations. *Violence and Victims, 23*, 133–155.

Matthews, D. (1995). *Foundations for violence free living*. St. Paul, MN: Amherst H. Wilder Foundation.

Mayfield, D., McLeod, G., & Hall, P. (1974). The CAGE questionnaire: Validation of a new alcoholism screening instrument. *The American Journal of Psychiatry, 131*, 1121–1123.

McCollum, E. E., & Stith, S. M. (2008). Couples treatment for IPV: A review of outcome research literature and current clinical practices. *Violence and Victims, 23*, 187–201.

McFarlane, W. R. (2005). Psychoeducational multifamily groups for families with persons with severe mental illlness. In J. Lebow (Ed.), *Handbook of clinical family therapy* (pp. 195–227). Hoboken, NJ: Wiley.

Meth, R. L. (1992). Marriage and family therapists working with family violence: Strained bedfellows or compatible partners? A commentary on Avis, Kaufman, and Bograd. *Journal of Marital and Family Therapy, 18*, 257–261.

Milardo, R. M. (1998). Gender asymmetry in common couple violence. *Personal Relationships, 5*, 423–438. doi:10.1111/j.1475-6811.1998.tb00180.x

Miller, W. R., & Rollnick, S. (2002). *Motivational interviewing: Preparing people to change addictive behavior* (2nd ed.). New York, NY: Guilford Press.

Minuchin, S., & Nichols, M. P. (1993). *Family healing: Strategies for hope and understanding*. New York, NY: Simon & Schuster.

Moore, T. M., & Stuart, G. L. (2004). Illicit substance use and intimate partner violence among men in batterers' intervention. *Psychology of Addictive Behaviors, 18*, 385–389. doi:10.1037/0893-164X.18.4.385

Novaco, R. W. (1975). *Anger control*. Lexington, MA: Lexington.

O'Leary, K. D., Heyman, R. E., & Neidig, P. H. (1999). Treatment of wife abuse: A comparison of gender-specific and conjoint approaches. *Behavior Therapy, 30*, 475–505. doi:10.1016/S0005-7894(99)80021-5

O'Leary, K. D., & Murphy, C. (1992). Clinical issues in the assessment of spouse abuse. In R. T. Ammerman & M. Hersen (Eds.), *Assessment of family violence: A clinical and legal sourcebook* (pp. 26–46). Wiley Series on Personality Processes. New York, NY: Wiley.

O'Leary, K. D., & Murphy, C. (1999). Clinical issues in the assessment of partner violence. In R. Ammersman & M. Hersen (Eds.), *Assessment of family violence: A clinical and legal sourcebook* (2nd ed., pp. 46–94). Wiley Series on Personality Processes. New York, NY: Wiley.

O'Leary, K. D., Vivian, D., & Malone, J. (1992). Assessment of physical aggression against women in marriage: The need for multimodal assessment. *Behavioral Assessment, 14,* 5–14.

Pan, H. S., Neidig, P. H., & O'Leary, K. D. (1994). Predicting mild and severe husband-to-wife physical aggression. *Journal of Consulting and Clinical Psychology, 62,* 975–981. doi:10.1037/0022-006X.62.5.975

Parks, G. A., Marlatt, G. A., Bowen, S. W., Dillworth, T. M., Witkiewitz, K., Larimer, M. E., . . . Meijer, L. (2003). The University of Washington Vipassana Meditation Research Project. *American Jails, 17,* 13–17.

Pichot, T., & Dolan, Y. M. (2003). *Solution-focused brief therapy: Its effective use in agency settings.* New York, NY: Haworth Press.

Rose, S., Bisson, J., Churchill, R., & Wessely, S. (2002). Psychological debriefing for preventing posttraumatic stress disorder (PTSD). *Cochrane Database of Systematic Reviews, 2,* CD000560.

Rosen, K. H., Matheson, J., Stith, S. M., & McCollum, E. E. (2003). Negotiated time-out: A de-escalation tool for couples. *Journal of Marital and Family Therapy, 29,* 291–298. doi:10.1111/j.1752-0606.2003.tb01207.x

Saunders, D. G. (1992). A typology of men who batter: Three types derived from cluster analysis. *American Journal of Orthopsychiatry, 62,* 264–275. doi:10.1037/h0079333

Schacht, R. L., Dimidjian, S., George, W. H., & Berns, S. B. (2009). Domestic violence assessment procedures among couple therapists. *Journal of Marital and Family Therapy, 35,* 47–59. doi:10.1111/j.1752-0606.2008.00095.x

Schumm, W. R., Nichols, C. W., Schectman, K. L., & Grigsby, C. C. (1983). Characteristics of responses to the Kansas Marital Satisfaction Scale by a sample of 84 married mothers. *Psychological Reports, 53,* 567–572.

Segal, Z. V., Williams, J. M. G., & Teasdale, J. D. (2002). *Mindfulness-based cognitive therapy for depression: A new approach to preventing relapse.* New York, NY: Guilford Press.

Shapiro, S. L., Carlson, L. E., Astin, J. A., & Freedman, B. (2006). Mechanisms of mindfulness. *Journal of Clinical Psychology, 62,* 373–386. doi:10.1002/jclp.20237

Siegel, D. J. (2007). *The mindful brain: Reflection and attunement in the cultivation of well-being.* New York, NY: Norton.

Simpson, L. E., Doss, B. D., Wheeler, J., & Christensen, A. (2007). Relationship violence among couples seeking therapy: Common couple violence or battering? *Journal of Marital and Family Therapy, 33,* 270–283. doi:10.1111/j.1752-0606.2007.00021.x

Skinner, H. (1982). The drug abuse screening test. *Addictive Behaviors, 7,* 363–371. doi:10.1016/0306-4603(82)90005-3

Sprenkle, D. H. (1994). Wife abuse through the lens of "systems theory." *The Counseling Psychologist, 22*, 589–602. doi:10.1177/0011000094224005

Stith, S. M., McCollum, E. E., Birkland, K. L., Ward, D., & Rosen, K. H. (2006). *A comparison of depressed and non-depressed partner-abusing men.* Unpublished manuscript, Virginia Tech—Northern Virginia Center, Falls Church, VA.

Stith, S. M., McCollum, E. E., Rosen, K. H., Locke, L., & Goldberg, P. (2005). Domestic violence focused couples treatment. In J. Lebow (Ed.), *Handbook of clinical family therapy* (pp. 406–430). New York, NY: Wiley.

Stith, S. M., Miller, M. L., Boyle, J., Swinton, J., Ratcliff, G. C., & McCollum, E. E. (in press). Making a difference in making miracles: Common snares in miracle question effectiveness. *Journal of Marital and Family Therapy.* Advance online publication. doi: 10.1111/j.1752-0606.2010.00207.x

Stith, S. M., Rosen, K. H., Barasch, S. G., & Wilson, S. M. (1991). Clinical research as a training opportunity: Bridging the gap between theory and practice. *Journal of Marital and Family Therapy, 17*, 349–353. doi:10.1111/j.1752-0606.1991.tb00904.x

Stith, S. M., Rosen, K. H., & McCollum, E. E. (1999). *Domestic violence focused couples treatment manual.* Unpublished manuscript, Virginia Tech, Falls Church, VA.

Stith, S. M., Rosen, K. H., & McCollum, E. E. (2002a). Developing a manualized couples treatment for domestic violence: Overcoming challenges. *Journal of Marital and Family Therapy, 28*, 21–25. doi:10.1111/j.1752-0606.2002.tb01168.x

Stith, S. M., Rosen, K. H., & McCollum, E. E. (2002b). Domestic violence. In D. H. Sprenkle (Ed.), *Effectiveness research in marriage and family therapy* (pp. 223–254). Alexandria, VA: American Association for Marriage and Family Therapy.

Stith, S. M., Rosen, K. H., McCollum, E. E., & Thomsen, C. J. (2004). Treating intimate partner violence within intact couple relationships: Outcomes of multicouple versus individual couple therapy. *Journal of Marital and Family Therapy, 30*, 305–318. doi:10.1111/j.1752-0606.2004.tb01242.x

Stith, S. M., & Straus, M. A. (1995). Introduction. In S. M. Stith & M. A. Straus (Eds.), *Understanding partner violence: Prevalence, causes, consequences, and solutions* (pp. 1–11). Minneapolis, MN: National Council on Family Relations.

Straus, M. A. (1993). Physical assaults by wives: A major social problem. In R. J. Gelles (Ed.), *Current controversies on family violence* (pp. 67–87). Newbury Park, CA: Sage.

Straus, M. A., Gelles, R. J., & Steinmetz, S. K. (1980). *Behind closed doors: Violence in the American family.* New York, NY: Doubleday/Anchor.

Straus, M. A., Hamby, S. L., Boney-McCoy, S., & Sugarman, D. B. (1996). The revised Conflict Tactics Scales (CTS2): Development and preliminary psychometric data. *Journal of Family Issues, 17*, 283–316. doi:10.1177/019251396017003001

Straus, M. A., & Yodanis, C. L. (1996). Corporal punishment in adolescence and physical assaults on spouses in later life: What accounts for the link? *Journal of Marriage and the Family, 58*, 825–841. doi:10.2307/353973

Stuart, G. L., & Holtzworth-Munroe, A. (1995). Identifying subtypes of maritally violent men: Descriptive dimensions, correlates and causes of violence, and treatment implications. In S. Stith & M. Straus (Eds.), *Understanding partner violence: Prevalence, causes, consequences, and solutions* (pp. 162–172). Minneapolis, MN: National Council on Family Relations.

Sullivan, C. M., Basta, J., Tan, C., & Davidson, W. S., II. (1992). After the crisis: A needs assessment of women leaving a domestic violence shelter. *Violence and Victims, 7,* 267–275.

Sullivan, C. M., & Rumptz, M. H. (1994). Adjustment and needs of African-American women who utilized a domestic violence shelter. *Violence and Victims, 9,* 275–286.

Todahl, J. L., Linville, D., Chou, L., & Cosenza, P. (2008). A qualitative study of intimate partner violence universal screening by family therapy interns: Implications for practice, research, training, and supervision. *Journal of Marital and Family Therapy, 34,* 28–43. doi:10.1111/j.1752-0606.2008.00051.x

Tjaden, P., & Thoennes, N. (1998). *Prevalence, incidence and consequences of violence against women* (Publication No. NCJ 172837). Washington, DC: National Institute of Justice.

Tolman, R. (1990). *The impact of group process on outcome of groups for men who batter.* Paper presented at the European Congress on the Advancement of Behavior Therapy, Paris, France.

Tucker, L. L., Stith, S. M., Howell, L. W., McCollum, E. E., & Rosen, K. H. (2000). Meta-dialogues in solution-oriented domestic violence focused couples treatment. *Journal of Systemic Therapies, 19,* 56–72.

U.S. Department of Justice. (2002). *Crime in the United States, 2001.* Washington, DC: Federal Bureau of Investigation.

Walker, L. E. (1979). *The battered woman.* New York, NY: Harper & Row.

Weiner-Davis, M., de Shazer, S., & Gingerich, W. (1987). Using pretreatment change to construct a therapeutic solution: A clinical note. *Journal of Marital and Family Therapy, 13,* 359–363. doi:10.1111/j.1752-0606.1987.tb00717.x

Weisz, A. N., Tolman, R. M., & Saunders, D. G. (2000). Assessing the risk of severe domestic violence: The importance of survivors' predictions. *Journal of Interpersonal Violence, 15,* 75–90. doi:10.1177/088626000015001006

Wile, D. B. (1993). *After the fight: Using your disagreements to build a stronger relationship.* New York, NY: Guilford Press.

Wileman, R., & Wileman, B. (1995). Towards balancing power in domestic violence relationships. *The Australian and New Zealand Journal of Family Therapy, 16,* 165–176.

Witkiewitz, K., Marlatt, G. A., & Walker, D. (2005). Mindfulness-based relapse prevention for alcohol and substance use disorders. *Journal of Cognitive Psychotherapy, 19,* 211–228. doi:10.1891/jcop.2005.19.3.211

Yalom, I. D. (1995). *The theory and practice of group psychotherapy* (4th ed.). New York, NY: Basic Books.

INDEX

Siegel, D. J., 77
Signaling (negotiated time-out), 95
Single-couple treatment
    overview, 48
    as part of treatment format, 37
    research on impact of, 171
    reviewing pretest data in, 66
SIP (Short Inventory of Problem),
    117
Situational couple violence, 14–15, 39
Skill deficits, 150
Skills, for dealing with violence, 75
Social comfort, 111
Social context, of domestic
    violence–focused couples
    therapy, 175
Social isolation, 68
Softened start-ups, 105–107
Solution-focused approach, 91, 141,
    147–151
Solution-focused brief therapy (SFBT),
    32–36
    appreciative stance in, 32–33
    asking questions in, 130
    as basis for domestic–violence
        focused couples therapy, 19
    and change, 47
    changing static descriptions to fluid
        descriptions in, 33–34
    clients' goals in, 34
    descriptions of solutions in, 33
    flexible approaches in, 34
    role of the future in, 132
    use of goals in, 129
Solution-Focused Brief Therapy
    Association, 32
Solutions
    descriptions of, 33
    development of, 129
Solution sequences, 137–138
Spiritual beliefs, 82. See also Religion
Sprenkle, D. H., 10
Stalking, 27
State guidelines, for offender treatment,
    9–10
Stith, S. M., 4
Strategic school of therapy, 137
Straus, M. A., 17
Strength, 33, 34, 145

Stress
    addressing stressful life circum-
        stances, 149–150
    management of, 157, 173
    mindfulness meditation for reducing,
        76, 77
    posttraumatic stress disorder,
        39–40, 124
    and presession check-ins, 125
    as risk factor, 39
Stressors, 70
Stuart, G. L., 13, 14
Substance abuse, 109–120. See also
        Alcohol and drug use (Session 6)
    as cause for exclusion from
        therapy, 29
    as constraint, 151
    and cooling off, 96
    couples therapy for treating, 11
    defined, 114
    ground rules prohibiting use of, 45
    mindfulness meditation for
        treatment of, 76–77
    as risk factor, 39
    screening for, 24, 25, 109, 110,
        114–115, 117–118
Substance abuse services, 30
Successes
    acknowledgment of clients',
        131–133, 142–145
    asking about, 125
    descriptions of, 33
    determining patterns that lead to,
        137–138
    taking note of small, 133–134
Suicidality, 27, 124
Systemic family therapists, 10
Systems theory, 10, 16

"Teach last" stance, 42
Termination, of conjoint therapy,
    157–158
Therapeutic alliance, 176, 177
Therapeutic interventions, 177–178
Therapeutic relationship, 176–177
Therapist–client interaction, 117–118,
    176–177
Therapist-directed approach, 40–42,
    59–60, 122
Therapists
    check-in process for, 126

ABOUT THE AUTHORS

Sandra M. Stith, PhD, LCMFT, is a professor and director of the marriage and family therapy program at Kansas State University. Her primary research interest is in understanding and treating intimate partner violence. She has edited three books on the subject, including *Understanding Partner Violence: Prevalence, Causes, Consequences and Solutions*, coedited with Dr. Murray Straus, and *Prevention of Intimate Partner Violence*. She publishes widely in the professional literature and has received funding, with Drs. McCollum and Rosen, from the National Institutes of Health to develop and test a couples treatment program for intimate partner violence. Dr. Stith has worked with the U.S. Air Force Family Advocacy Program since 1998, managing and conducting a variety of family violence–related research projects. In 2004 she received the American Association for Marriage and Family Therapy's Outstanding Contribution to Marriage and Family Therapy Award, and in 2007 she received the American Family Therapy Association's Distinguished Contribution to Family Systems Research Award and Kansas State University's Distinguished Alumni Award.

Eric E. McCollum, PhD, LCSW, LMFT, is a professor in and program director of the marriage and family therapy master's program at Virginia Tech. He had a 15-year clinical career, including 12 years as a staff member of the Menninger Clinic in Topeka, Kansas, before beginning his academic career in 1989 as a faculty member in the marriage and family therapy doctoral program at Purdue University. His academic interests include the treatment of intimate partner violence and the use of mindfulness meditation in treatment and in the training of therapists. In addition to his many contributions to the professional literature, he has published two prior books, *Family Solutions for Substance Abuse* with Terry Trepper and *More Than Miracles: The State of the Art of Solution-Focused Brief Therapy* with Steve de Shazer, Yvonne Dolan, Harry Korman, Terry Trepper, and Insoo Kim Berg. He is coeditor with Cynthia Franklin, Terry Trepper, and Wallace Gingerich of the forthcoming *Solution-Focused Brief Therapy: From Practice to Research–Informed Practice*. In 2008, Dr. McCollum received the American Association for Marriage and Family Therapy's Training Award.

Karen H. Rosen, EdD, was a faculty member in the marriage and family therapy master's program at Virginia Tech for more than 15 years. Before that, she was a clinician and supervisor and directed the training clinic at Virginia Tech. Her academic interests lay in the area of understanding and treating intimate partner violence. Primarily a qualitative researcher, she was the author of many professional papers and one book, *Violence Hits Home: Comprehensive Treatment Approaches to Domestic Violence* with Sandra Stith and Mary Beth Williams. At the time of her death in 2008, Dr. Rosen was professor emeritus at Virginia Tech.